A CAMBRIDGE TOPIC BOOK

The London Police
in the Nineteenth Century

John Wilkes

Published in cooperation with Cambridge University Press
Lerner Publications Company, Minneapolis

Editors' Note: All references to money in this book are given in British monetary units. During the middle years of the nineteenth century, the basic unit, the pound (£), was worth 20 shillings (s) or 240 pence (d). In this period, one pound was worth between four and five American dollars.

LIBRARY OF CONGRESS CATALOGING IN PUBLICATION DATA

Wilkes, John, 1937-
  The London Police in the nineteenth century.

  (A Cambridge topic book)
  Includes index.
  Summary: Describes the establishment of the Metropolitan Police force by Sir Robert Peel, the principles on which it operated, the recruitment and working conditions throughout the nineteenth century, and public reaction to this law enforcement body.
  1. Great Britain. Metropolitan Police Office—History—19th century—Juvenile literature. 2. Police—England—London—History—19th century—Juvenile literature. [1. Police—England—London—History—19th century. 2. Great Britain. Metropolitan Police Office—History—19th century] I. Title.
HV8196.L6W54   1984   363.2'09421   84-17122
ISBN 0-8225-1233-5 (lib. bdg.)

This edition first published in 1984 by Lerner Publications Company by permission of Cambridge University Press.

Original edition copyright © 1977 by Cambridge University Press as part of *The Cambridge Introduction to the History of Mankind: Topic Book.*

International Standard Book Number 0-8225-1233-5
Library of Congress Catalog Card Number: 84-17122

Manufactured in the United States of America

This edition is available exclusively from:
Lerner Publications Company, 241 First Avenue North, Minneapolis, Minnesota 55401

1 2 3 4 5 6 7 8 9 92 91 90 89 88 87 86 85 84

Contents

1 Old watchman to 'new police'

If you had been standing in Whitehall, London, just after 6 p.m. on the evening of 9 September 1829, you would have seen something quite new: a line of men in tall hats and long blue coats marching along the street. Every so often a man would turn smartly off to left or right, and begin his job of pounding up and down a little group of streets all night long. You would have seen the very first patrol made by the Metropolitan Police. This book is about the policemen of London from 1829 to a time just before the First World War.

right: *William Anthony, the last London watchman. As the new police stations were built, old watch-houses, like this one in Lambeth, became private dwellings.*

Before the police

The police are so much a part of city life nowadays that it is hard to imagine how London could ever have carried on without them. But the truth is that before 1829 there was very little protection for ordinary folk in country or town. They depended on the parish constables (who were not professional police) and, in the towns, on the watchmen who for centuries had had the job of patrolling the streets at night. The watchmen, who were nicknamed 'Charleys', were supposed to catch criminals, but were often so old and feeble that they had no chance of success. They generally preferred a quiet walk up and down, calling out the hours, and long rests in their huts.

This system gave many criminals a very good living. Robberies and attacks were so common that as a matter of course people often went about with some weapon, even if it was only a strong stick.

From time to time ideas were put forward to try to make London safer. The men who did most were the magistrates at Bow Street. A magistrate (or J.P., for Justice of the Peace) is a sort of judge. He has the power to issue an order, called a 'warrant', for someone to be arrested, or for a house to be entered and searched. He also has the right to swear-in men to carry out those orders.

The Bow Street magistrates had such a body of men, who came to be called the 'Bow Street Runners'. Most were what we should now describe as detectives. The London magistrates also had bands of uniformed men, who patrolled some of the approaches to London. These were useful groups, though too few: only about 350 in all, and not well organized. Some of the Bow Street Runners were corrupt. A favourite trick was to allow a crime to take place, then to tell the victim they had been able to recover the property. He would then pay them the usual, legal reward. But then the Runners would gain a *second* reward by informing on the man whom they knew to have done the crime. A better disciplined and more effective organization than this was now becoming necessary.

2 The need for a police force

Why was a police force needed? The idea was not new, but for years people had resisted it; we shall see why near the end of this chapter. But now there were so many changes and new problems that the whole matter had to be thought out again. The reasons *why* the Metropolitan Police Force was founded in 1829, and why it was organized in a particular way, came from the needs of London. Nineteenth-century London was a very special city, a mixture of many different places and peoples, sometimes linked, sometimes separate. You need to know something about it in order to understand the task of the police. In many ways the city and the people have not changed much, and quite a lot of modern police work still rests on the foundations laid in 1829.

London – the changing city

The first reason why London needed better policing than before was because it was becoming much bigger. It had over one million inhabitants in 1801. By 1851 there were about two million, and by 1901 about six million. This was due partly to natural increase (for London had many young people and a high birthrate) but still more to immigration.

Newcomers poured into London every day. The map shows where they came from. You can see that in the early part of the century most immigrants came from the rural counties around London. They were mostly farm labourers; these people had the difficult task of finding jobs in different trades, though there was still some agriculture in London until almost the end of the century. We know that between 1841 and 1851 at least one Londoner in six was an immigrant. By the middle of the century immigrants were coming from further afield, as the map shows. Scots, Welsh and especially Irish came in large numbers all through the century, with an Irish peak around the famine years of the 1840s. At the end of our period immigrants came from still further away. These were Central

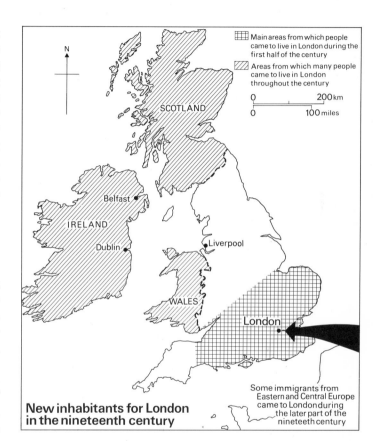

New inhabitants for London in the nineteenth century

Main areas from which people came to live in London during the first half of the century

Areas from which many people came to live in London throughout the century

0   200 km
0   100 miles

Some immigrants from Eastern and Central Europe came to London during the later part of the nineteenth century

and Eastern Europeans, mainly Jews, fleeing from poverty and brutal persecution.

The East End: docks and railways

Immigrants and native-born Londoners alike had to live within walking distance of their work and in places where the rent was not too high. There was industry of one kind or another

5

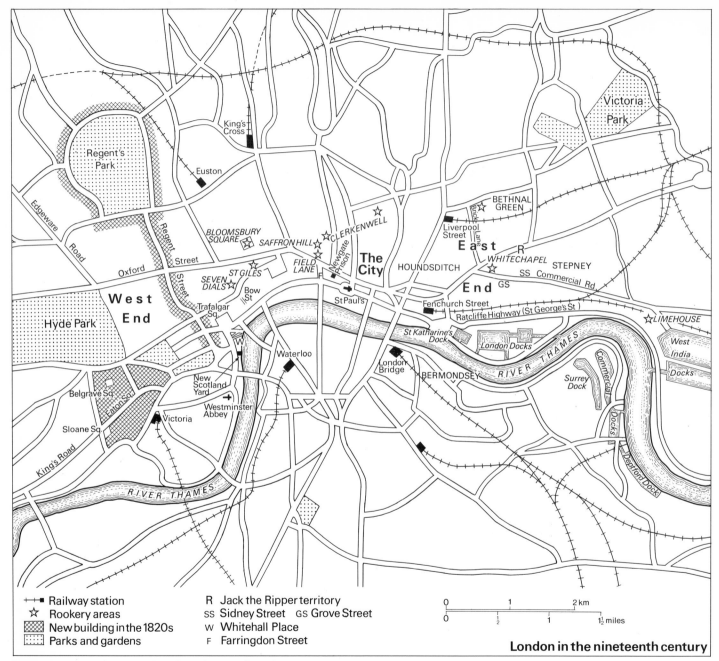

London in the nineteenth century

This is a composite map showing places referred to in the book as they were at that time.
In this period London was constantly changing.

almost everywhere in London, though this type of work was mostly to be found in the East End. The districts close to the Thames were especially crowded. When the building of the London docks began at the turn of the century (the West India dock was opened in 1802) the overcrowding became very much worse. The great sailing ships unloaded their cargoes of sugar, rum and indigo directly onto quays protected by twenty-foot walls. Goods were stored in acres of brick-built warehouses and cellars.

The new docks took up a vast amount of space. Some was marshy ground, which had never been anything but rough pasture; other areas had been lived in for generations. Hundreds of houses were knocked down and the inhabitants driven into other parts of the East End. Not only did these people suffer, but the districts they moved into were dragged down by the overcrowding and became slums. (The word 'slum' dates from about the 1820s.) St Katherine's Dock, for example, made 11,300 Stepney people homeless.

After the docks came the railways. Every railway company wanted to bring a line into the heart of London to link up with the new docks, wherever possible, and to be able to build a grand terminus, or station, which all would see and admire.

Some of the buildings, especially at Euston (about 1840), were very fine, but the cost was enormous. You could say it was the poor who paid. The building of a railway was a huge job. Thousands of labourers descended on London, demolishing, tunnelling, building. The companies tried to get land cheaply and to go through the poorest districts. Working people were

Excavating St Katharine's Dock in 1828, from a contemporary picture. The Tower of London is in the background.

dislodged, just as they had been when the docks were built. Tenants were offered a pound or two, sometimes less, to go. The smoke and steam of railways, the goods yards and coal dumps, made railway districts very unpleasant to live in, and only the poorest remained. Look at the areas surrounding all modern termini, except one, and you can still see the effects of steam railways. The exception is Victoria. The powerful Duke of Westminster would not allow goods traffic there, and kept the railway company under control, so that his magnificent properties were not spoiled. Other areas were not so lucky.

The docks and the railways, then, made housing for poor people in the East End and parts of North London even scarcer than it had been at the beginning of the century. Workmen's cheap rail fares, which made it possible to think about living away from the slum and still being able to get to work, did not begin until the 1860s. Overcrowding, and lack of almost every service that present-day city-dwellers take for granted, made life in these areas hard indeed.

Crime and the poor

Honest men and criminals alike were packed together in the slums of East London: Clerkenwell, St Giles, Stepney, the Ratcliffe Highway, Bermondsey. A room shared with up to six or eight people became home for most of the newcomers. Immigrants also tended to stay with those who had once lived in the same place as themselves: the Irish in St Giles in the first half of the century, and Jews in Whitechapel near the end, are both good examples. Criminals also liked to live together, especially in places which were so full of narrow, twisting, crowded alleys that they could slip quickly away from any pursuer.

Everyone who lived in such areas spent much more time out of his house than we do today. A foul room, in a tumble-down house built without running water or sewers, gave no pleasure. Men and women alike went to beer shops, or pubs, or simply watched the world go by. Children were everywhere. Compulsory schooling did not come in until 1870. Many city children did not go to school before (and after) that year, mainly because their parents needed the few pennies a child could pick up. Children did casual work: errands, sweeping street-crossings, being a bootblack. Others were put into factories, or worked at home, from age ten, or sometimes earlier.

Cruikshank's cartoon of 1828 from Scraps and Sketches shows the hard life which even an honest working family could expect in a London slum.

Shopping took up much time in the nineteenth century. The poor dealt mainly with street traders and small local shops, which in turn had to get their stock from markets or from the producers. The big chain-stores of present day cities, with their pre-packed preserved groceries and meats, were a hundred years in the future: in nineteenth-century cities fresh food had to be bought daily. Vegetable venders had their wheelbarrows, as did clothes merchants, haberdashers, flower sellers and many others. Some people had specialities: Italians were hurdy-gurdy men (ice-cream came later), Irish girls sold oranges, Jews second-hand clothes. 'Ol' cloes' was East End slang for a Jew at one time.

Crime fitted into this way of life. It was usually small-scale but there was a very great deal of it. Criminals went for everyday things they could sell second-hand, as well as for money and valuables.

We have a list of London crimes and criminals for 1837, after the police were set up. The actual figures are very unreliable, because we cannot say how much crime was not reported to the police, but they give an idea of the sort of law-breaking that went on.

4,500	thieves and robbers
2,700	disturbers of the peace, drunks, brawlers, etc.
800	pickpockets
1,000	vagrants, tramps, travelling and homeless people
400	frauds and con-men, some street criminals
5,800	prostitutes.

Many of these committed crimes because they lived a hard life and were very short of money. Others were professionals. Pickpockets were usually small boys, whose nimble fingers had not been ruined by hard labour in prison. They were trained by older thieves and often worked in gangs, with 'stalls' who distracted attention while the boy went swiftly for a gold watch or fat wallet. An unlucky man might have his watch stolen at one end of a street and find himself buying it back at the other. On a dark night in rougher districts there would sometimes be violence, leaving a man stripped naked (since all his clothes could be sold) and perhaps injured as well. Drunks were popular victims. The streets were also full of prostitutes, whose presence annoyed 'respectable' people.

Confidence men ('mags-men') had a variety of tricks. 'Find-the-lady', or the three card trick, was a favourite. Others specialized in finding some innocent who had just arrived in London and luring him into a rigged card game. Cheap lodging houses often contained someone who could spot a newcomer and cheat him while pretending to help him find a job. False beggars were very common.

The really professional and successful criminals did not operate on the streets. They might live in the middle of a slum, operating as coiners or forgers, or running a lodging house which served to train boys for thieving, or receiving stolen goods, or writing very cunning begging letters. Others would travel about the country on railway trains, stealing from hotels and in places where they were not known. London gangs were well organized to receive and resell stolen goods.

The West End

Crime and violence on the streets stayed mainly in the East End. The larger robberies moved outside. Just as changes in the East End affected the life of the people, and crime, so a new look was coming to the West End also. Some Londoners

'Thimble-rigging', a form of the three card trick, provided an easier living than a workshop. The clothes of the rigger and his 'mark' show who was the newcomer to the city. From the Illustrated London News, *1842.*

were becoming very rich, and many others were making more money than ever before. The profits of trade, banking, building and industry were ready to spend. There was a demand for splendid houses and brilliant shops. Landowners began to create estates. The greatest of these was the Crown, and we are lucky that the ruler of England in the 1820s was George IV, formerly the Prince Regent, one of the few English kings who has been really interested in art and architecture. With his architect, John Nash, George planned a marvellous 'garden city', near the royal park (now called Regent's Park). The whole plan was never carried out, but Regent Street was built between 1817 and 1823. A little later the Regent made Buckingham House into a royal palace, and improved the district around.

The Duke of Westminster used earth from St Katherine's Dock to fill in some marshy ground near the King's Road, in Chelsea. The earth, which had supported a Stepney slum, now carried the weight of the magnificent squares and streets running from Sloane Square to Victoria Station. George Basevi

Hanover Terrace was part of the Prince Regent's plan for north-west London. Compare the life of the family here with that of the cobbler, on page 8.

and Thomas Cubitt built Belgrave and Eaton Squares, and mews houses for horses and servants. The whole district is still called Belgravia.

There were other developments in London, all creating new and very expensive properties, filled with valuable things. Casks of rum in a West India Dock warehouse, diamonds glittering at an Eaton Square dinner party, stacks of sovereigns in a City bank, each attracted envy and theft. So people who had a lot (or even a little) began to look around for protection from thieves and rioters.

Revolution and freedom

We can now see why the Prime Minister, the Duke of Wellington, and his government were worried about crime in the streets, and the danger to people and property all over a great city. But there had been complaints about lack of protection for many, many years previously. One reason why the docks had been built was to protect the valuable goods coming into England. It was the West India merchants who paid, as they had paid for a River Police from 1798. Poorer people were equally at risk. Gangs of over a hundred men were known in Bethnal Green, forcing shopkeepers to stay shut and shuttered. The Ratcliffe Highway, near the port of London, had seen a whole series of murders. Why was nothing done until 1829?

A very important reason was that a great many people did not *want* a police force. The English were not used to being ordered about. There was no elaborate system of local government with its officials and regulations, and not much interference from the national government. Civil servants were neither numerous nor powerful. Everyone looked after himself, if he could, and the laws were mainly intended to stop violence and theft while people got on with their own business. Punishment was often severe if a man was caught breaking the law, but the chances of getting away were very big. Honest people accepted this because they feared that the government would use a police force not just to catch criminals, but also to crush opposition and make itself too powerful. Most Englishmen thought that France was already an oppressive state, full of government spies and agents. They said that it was better to put up with a few more criminals in a free country than risk a tyranny. These were reasons why all

sorts of people opposed the idea of a police force, though others could see the need for something to be done. By 1829 there were enough of these to get Parliament to agree to set up a police force, if it was properly controlled.

The second reason why action was taken in 1829 was because the government and others were frightened that a revolution might come in England. For several years some writers and speakers had been demanding a reform of Parliament. Some saw this as meaning that there would be a revolution. We know now that no revolution was brewing but this was not realized at the time. The government also remembered France, where the people of the Paris slums had risen up in 1789, taken the Bastille fortress and set off the French Revolution. Perhaps there were conspirators in the London slums, waiting for the moment when they could come pouring out into Westminster and storm the Houses of Parliament? After all, the rich and respectable never went into the slums, and had no idea what was going on.

Also, the government remembered the year 1780, when the London mob *had* broken loose. A mad nobleman – Lord George Gordon – whipped them up to hate Catholics. Some came out of Seven Dials, in St Giles, and Clerkenwell to burn Catholic houses and steal property. Others used the 'Gordon riots' as cover for all sorts of crimes, including breaking into Newgate Prison and letting out their friends and relations.

It took the army to put down the Gordon riots. No one liked using soldiers for such jobs. They were not trained for them. They were trained to use their weapons, and if they did this they could kill many unarmed people very quickly. This might enrage others so that riots became worse and would need even more violence to put them down. Soldiers could not be used to patrol every day, or freedom might really disappear. A force was needed which was disciplined, but not military.

These, then, were the reasons why the British Parliament was ready to try out a police force. London was so big and changing so fast that it seemed almost out of control. Rich and poor needed protection for their lives and property; a great city, full of valuable things, had to be looked after. Some thought at the time that a police force might also be needed to stop revolutions.

3   Sir Robert Peel and the 'new police'

The man who planned the 'new police', as they were called at the time, was Sir Robert Peel. He became Home Secretary in 1822. The Home Secretary was (and is) an important government minister. He was responsible for law and order, though he had many other jobs. He was not a judge or any sort of policeman himself, being an elected member of the House of Commons, or a peer. Peel was such a politician, and later became Prime Minister.

Peel made a good reply to those who said that the new police would take away liberty. He said, 'I want to teach people that liberty does not consist in having your house robbed by organized gangs of thieves, and in leaving the principal streets of London in the nightly possession of drunken women and vagabonds.' Nevertheless, he had to be very careful not to upset too many people. The bill for the police went through Parliament without much trouble, though Peel had to leave the City of London out of his plans, as we shall see.

Peel decided that he would set up a force of uniformed men. He also chose to have his men patrolling the streets, rather than waiting at the police station until a crime was reported and going out then, or spying in plain clothes. He wanted the sight of a policeman to help *prevent* crime. Of course the police were to catch criminals once a crime was committed, but the idea of preventing it came first and foremost.

A policeman was most likely to prevent crime, and catch criminals, if he knew the area where he worked very well. So the police used the 'beat' system. Every constable had a fixed area which he had to patrol. The policeman had to get to know who was who on his beat. And people would see *him*. The sight of the uniform would remind honest men that they had protection, and criminals that the law was always close at hand, so that the arm of the law could quickly be on their collar. The police were to become familiar figures, walking slowly so that anyone had time to speak to them, and being a part of the landscape. There were to be no 'French' spies or bullying soldiers.

Setting up the force

Peel's first job was to choose who should be the Commissioners, the name given to the chief policemen. He chose Charles Rowan and Richard Mayne. They will be described later in this book. Rowan and Mayne drew up a plan (which Peel approved) on how the force was to be organized. The diagram shows this plan, though it was not carried out in every detail. The exact number of officers and constables varied between divisions. Some parts of the Metropolitan Police Force were not set up until after 1829. These will be described later.

The authorized strength ('establishment') of the police was to be 2,800, but 3,314 men were actually recruited by the

Sir Robert Peel (1788– 1850) founder of the Metropolitan Police. He was Home Secretary from 1822, and afterwards a Conservative Prime Minister. The painting is by J. Linnell, 1838.

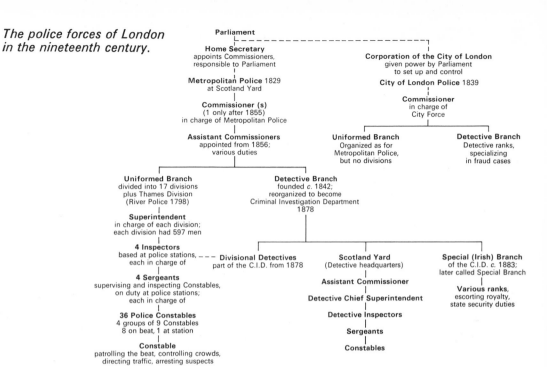

The police forces of London in the nineteenth century.

Parliament

Home Secretary
appoints Commissioners,
responsible to Parliament

Corporation of the City of London
given power by Parliament
to set up and control

Metropolitan Police 1829
at Scotland Yard

City of London Police 1839

Commissioner (s)
(1 only after 1855)
in charge of Metropolitan Police

Commissioner
in charge of
City Force

Assistant Commissioners
appointed from 1856;
various duties

Uniformed Branch
Organized as for
Metropolitan Police,
but no divisions

Detective Branch
Detective ranks,
specializing
in fraud cases

Uniformed Branch
divided into 17 divisions
plus Thames Division
(River Police 1798)

Detective Branch
founded *c.* 1842;
reorganized to become
Criminal Investigation Department
1878

Superintendent
in charge of each division;
each division had 597 men

4 Inspectors
based at police stations,
each in charge of

Divisional Detectives
part of the C.I.D. from 1878

Scotland Yard
(Detective headquarters)

Special (Irish) Branch
of the C.I.D. *c.* 1883;
later called Special Branch

4 Sergeants
supervising and inspecting Constables,
on duty at police stations;
each in charge of

Assistant Commissioner

Various ranks,
escorting royalty,
state security duties

Detective Chief Superintendent

36 Police Constables
4 groups of 9 Constables
8 on beat, 1 at station

Detective Inspectors

Sergeants

Constable
patrolling the beat, controlling crowds,
directing traffic, arresting suspects

Constables

---

middle of 1830. In 1839 the River Police were taken into the Metropolitan Police as Thames Division, and are still responsible for patrolling London's river.

The City

This left only one part of London outside Metropolitan Police control: the City of London itself.

The City is in the heart of London, and is only about one square mile in area. It seems obvious that the Metropolitan Police should work there. However, the City was a very special square mile. For centuries it had had its own local government, with a Lord Mayor and Aldermen elected by the merchants and shopkeepers. The City Corporation was answerable to no man except the king, and *he* was not much interested in their affairs. The great bankers and traders, many of whom still lived in the City, were very powerful. As well as controlling much of the finance of the whole country they had supporters and dependents in both Houses of Parliament. The City could, and did, block any Parliamentary bill which it thought might take away its freedom, or increase the rates. Its in-habitants, by and large, intended to look after their own interests and saw no reason why they should fit in with the rest of London. The City was so powerful that Peel had had to leave it out of his police bill. The Metropolitan Police had no powers there at all.

Even so, the City had to do something, otherwise every criminal would simply move into the City so as to get away from the Metropolitan Police. Very slowly, always protesting, it reformed and expanded its own force of 'Charleys'. This was not enough. In 1839 it set up a proper force under a Commissioner, Daniel Whittle Harvey.

Although the City force was not large – about 500 men at the beginning – it operated in the same way as the Metropolitan Police, took a roughly similar uniform, maintained fierce discipline, and co-operated with the Metropolitan when it was necessary. The two forces did the same kind of work under about the same conditions.

By 1840 all London was policed. The forces could operate over an area of 15 miles (24 km) radius from Charing Cross, and as new suburbs were built for the growing population of London, they came under control from the beginning.

4 'Peel's bloody gang'

In this chapter we shall look mostly at the Uniformed Branch of the police. The examples given and the policemen mentioned by name are all from real life, although they come from different periods of the nineteenth century. That does not matter much, because the job that uniformed policemen did, and the way they did it, hardly changed between 1829 and the end of the century. Of course conditions of work and the life of London altered greatly, but this affected the police less than you might think. We shall go down the ranks, starting at the top.

The Commissioners

As we saw on the diagram on page 13, the chief policemen of London were called Commissioners. These men had the same

Sir Charles Rowan (1783–1852), Commissioner 1829–50. This portrait, by William Salter, shows him in military uniform.

Sir Richard Mayne (1796–1868), Commissioner 1829–68. This portrait was engraved from a photograph.

powers as magistrates, though they never sat in court. The success or failure of the 'new police' in 1829 depended on the two men Peel had chosen. What sort of men were they?

Colonel Charles Rowan was a forty-six-year-old bachelor. He had led an infantry regiment against Napoleon's Imperial Guard at the battle of Waterloo (1815) where he had been wounded. Richard Mayne was an Irish lawyer, the son of a judge, made Commissioner at the age of thirty-three. He had practised as a barrister in the north of England. He provided the law, and Rowan the order, although in later years Mayne became much harder than his fellow Commissioner.

The Commissioners worked well enough together until Rowan retired in 1850. Another soldier, Captain Hay, was appointed Joint Commissioner with Mayne, but the two men did not get on well and from 1855 Mayne was in sole charge. From that time there has been only one Commissioner, the highest rank in the Metropolitan Police. Richard Mayne was one of the greatest of the Commissioners. Inspector Cavanagh described him as he was after twenty-eight years as Commissioner, in 1857:

'He was sixty-three, about five feet eight inches, spare, but well-built, thin face, a very hard compressed mouth, grey hair and whiskers, an eye like that of a hawk. He was frequently at work from ten in the morning till late at night, himself answering most of the letters received and super-intending the most important of the departments of the office.'

Cavanagh goes on:

'I was ushered into his presence, and shall never forget the sensation I felt. He continued writing while I stood to attention for I should say ten minutes, each minute making me feel more uneasy and uncomfortable... his glance seemed to go right through me. At length, he said "Mr Yardley has

THE BOYS IN THE SNOW.—DRAWN BY JOHN LEECH. 1855

'Boys in the snow'
A cartoon by Leech in 1855 shows
the police uniform at that time.
The picture on the next page shows
how the uniform changed after
1865.

recommended you for promotion to the accountant's office. It is a very important position. I hope you will give him satisfaction." I bowed and left the room, a weight being lifted as I got outside the door...'

Rowan and Mayne were both 'gentlemen', that is to say they came from those small groups of well-born, wealthy, educated men who ruled Britain. All other nineteenth-century Commissioners (and Assistant Commissioners when they were appointed from 1856) came from the same background, and had previously been soldiers, lawyers or senior civil servants.

Other ranks

All other London policemen were recruited from what were then called 'the lower classes'. The senior appointments in 1829, especially to be Superintendent of a division, went mainly to ex-army N.C.O.s. Sergeant Major May was the first Superintendent of 'A' Division. He helped recruit the lower ranks, and taught riding and drill. For many years he was a key man, working directly under the Commissioners as if he was still a regimental sergeant major and they were colonels.

Men such as May usually had little schooling, but they were used to a disciplined life and to being in charge of others. Many of those who joined were also ex-servicemen.

Inspectors, sergeants and constables were recruited during 1829 and 1830 as the seventeen divisions were gradually manned. We do not have an account of 'joining up' from a very early recruit, but things were not much different from those days when Constable Cavanagh (later to rise to Chief Inspector) joined in 1855. In his *Memoirs* he describes what happened when he put on his new blue uniform:

'When I looked at myself in the glass with the uniform on for the first time, I wondered what could have led me to take the final step of becoming a "peeler". I had to put on a swallow-tail coat, and a rabbit-skin high top hat, covered with leather, weighing eighteen ounces; a pair of Wellington boots, the leather of which must have been at least a sixteenth of an inch thick, and a belt about four inches broad, with a great brass buckle some six inches deep...My hat was slipping all over my head; my boots which were two sizes too large, were rubbing the skin off my heels; and the stock was a thick leathern one, and four inches deep, was nearly

choking me. I would have given all I possessed to have got back into my ordinary clothes.'

Things improved when the police changed to helmet and tunic, about 1865, though the policeman lost his lunchbox when his topper was taken away.

Recruits were given two sets of uniform, often of very poor quality, a cape, an armlet to show when they were on duty, a lantern holder (later a 'bulls-eye' lantern), a rattle (whistles came in in 1884) and a truncheon made of hardwood. Each policeman was issued with a cutlass, but this was never carried on ordinary patrols. From that day to this no policeman on ordinary duties has carried a firearm.

Why did men join the police?

Cavanagh gives the most common reason. 'I had been out of employment for a long time, and made up my mind to get into the Police...or take the Queen's shilling. I was fortunate enough, with thirty-six others out of 140 applications, to get on.' Others might join because they liked the disciplined out-door life. Some were policemen's sons.

The Metropolitan Police did not have recruiting problems in the nineteenth century, though, for reasons we shall soon find out, a good many men left after a short while. Police life had many advantages, as well as some great drawbacks.

The biggest advantage in a police career was security. Although Britain was developing many large new industries in the nineteenth century there was always widespread un-employment. This was because the population was increasing and because men were moving out of the country districts to look for work in the cities. Much work was seasonal and people would be turned away after the harvest, or whenever demand in their industry fell. Dismissal could come at any time with no appeal. There was no unemployment or sickness pay, no help with rent or food, and trade unions were not strong enough to defend workers' interests until late in the nineteenth century, sometimes not then. A policeman could at least reckon that he stood a greater chance of eating more regularly (though not better) than many of those around him. There was also the prospect of a pension, which might keep him out of the workhouse in old age.

Secondly, a policeman was 'respectable'. That meant much to some ordinary people in Victorian times, though less than nothing to others.

Thirdly, a man might have the chance of a career. In order to understand what that meant we must look at police pay and promotion. Police pay is described later in this book; all we need to know now is that it was low, and not just because Peel wanted to save money.

Peel wanted some sorts of men, but not others, in the police, and he tried to set pay that would shut out those he did not want. He explained what he was trying to do in a letter to a friend called J. W. Croker. Croker had told Peel that a good type of man would not join for 3 shillings a day, which was what the police offered in 1829. Peel replied:

'No doubt three shillings a day will not give me all the virtues under heaven but I do not want them. Angels would be far above my work. I have refused to employ gentlemen – commissioned officers for instance – as superintendents and inspectors, because I am certain they would refuse to associate with other persons holding the same offices who were not of equal rank, and they would therefore degrade the latter in the eyes of the men.'

By 'equal rank' Peel means what we call 'social class', not military or police rank. He goes on:

'A sergeant of the Guards at £200 a year is a better man for my purpose than a captain of high military reputation if he would serve for nothing...a three shilling a day man is better than a five shilling a day man.'

By setting pay so low Peel cut out all those who might have upset discipline in the police force by giving themselves airs, or those who would have used the police as a dumping ground for their poor relations or servants, or army officers on pension, who would have tried to take all the senior jobs for themselves. We know Peel was really worried about this because he wrote to the Duke of Wellington saying so:

'The chief danger will be if it is made a *job*, if gentleman's servants and so forth are placed in the higher offices. I must frame regulations to guard against this...'

Peel's plan worked very well. The police force came from the working classes, who joined in large numbers in spite of the low pay. One reason was that the police force offered a career.

All police posts, except the Commissioners', were filled by promotion from the ranks. Most policemen spent their working lives as constables because, as the diagram on page 13 shows, there were far fewer sergeants and ranks above than there were constables. Nevertheless a constable who had the necessary education and common sense, plus a faultless conduct sheet, would serve for perhaps four or five years before being 'made up' to sergeant, and a further eight to ten years before becoming an inspector. He would then be earning roughly as much as a highly skilled craftsman or a clerk, though sometimes the police did better than people such as these, and sometimes worse. In the same way it took longer to be promoted at some periods than others, depending on how many inspectors and sergeants retired or died. The very best policemen could rise by seniority and merit to be Superintendents. There were only about twenty-five such posts in the whole Metropolitan Police.

Commissioners were appointed 'from the top', that is, directly by the Home Secretary. Very few nineteenth-century Commissioners or Assistant Commissioners had had any professional police experience before being appointed. Control of the force was kept firmly in the hands of what we might call the 'upper classes'. Nowadays this might be considered unfair, but it was the usual arrangement in Britain before the twentieth century and it seemed to work.

The system did give a chance of a career to a man who would otherwise have been a farm labourer or a factory hand. A Superintendent earned about £200 a year. This was comfortable, though not more, and about as much as a senior insurance clerk might earn. Yet it was a real move up for anyone who had started as a constable on the beat, and it gave an ordinary man a good deal of power. It is also true that if policemen had had the chance of being made Commissioners, then very few would have been suitable or happy. They had not education enough to cope with the complicated paper work. They would have found it hard to mix with the rich and famous, as Commissioners sometimes did. In an age where rank and family counted for far more than they do today, a commissioner from the ranks might have been ignored and treated rudely, or he might have been afraid to allow influential people to be questioned or suspected. That would have been dangerous for all the police.

There were two other ways in which a London policeman might be promoted. One was to transfer to the Detective Branch, where pay and promotion prospects were a little better than in the Uniformed Branch. The other was to leave the Metropolitan Police and go into senior posts in the county and borough forces, which were being set up all over the country, as the success of the London police became obvious to people in other towns and counties.

Hardships of the job

The disadvantages of police work were many. It was physically very hard: twenty miles a night, in all weathers, seven days a week. A constable might have to attend court after being on the beat all night, lose his sleep and still have to patrol the following night as usual. Until the year 1900 there were no official break-times allowed during a beat, and no hot meals. If a man became soaked and frozen at the beginning of a winter night, then he usually stayed that way until dawn.

Nineteenth-century London was a very unhealthy place in which to work. Open sewers and impure water led to cholera and many other diseases. Men had little resistance to chest diseases; tuberculosis killed more police than any number of thugs. London was a city whose houses, factories and railways burned smoky coal, causing the terrible winter fogs called 'London peculiars'. Constant patrolling in heavy, unsuitable boots injured the feet and legs.

The police themselves knew full well what was happening. In 1856, for example, the City of London Police Surgeon reported that many men were being worn out by the job. He wrote:

'By the term "Worn Out" made use of in my Certificates I would wish to imply that such Officers…are prematurely aged and suffer from defective physical strength and other bodily infirmities.'

This was in spite of the fact that when recruited they had 'a high standard of health and were capable of more than an ordinary amount of physical exertion'.

Pay

Though a policeman who was not sick or undisciplined was sure of work, his pay was very low. Superintendents were paid £200 a year, inspectors £100, sergeants about £58 and police constables £54 12s (£54.60), a year or 3 shillings (15p) a day. In 1829 a police constable in the City force could earn

The police were expected to enforce hard laws against the poor. Homeless people are being 'moved on' in St James's Park. You can read more about this aspect of police work on page 24.

A Sunday morning market in Lambeth. Street life mixed up honest and criminal folk. There are three policemen here, keeping a sharp lookout. Both these pictures are from the Illustrated London News *in the 1870s.*

as little as 17s 6d (87½p) a week, when all deductions had been made.

In 1868 a writer named R. D. Baxter made a list of occupations and wages. He put police wages at between 15 shillings (75p) and £1 per week. Actual pay in London was probably a little higher, but the list lets us compare police pay with that of other working men. Policemen, sailors, quarrymen, gamekeepers and civil service messengers were all at about the same level. The police earned more than farm labourers (which many would have been if they followed their father's trade) at 14 shillings (70p), but less than many working men; tailors, coalheavers, miners, postmen and railway workmen all took home about 22 shillings (£1.10). The best paid workers, highly skilled jewellery makers and instrument makers, and railway engine drivers, were paid 35 shillings (£1.75) a week.

The police found it harder to live than many of those who earned about the same money. This was because they were required to live near their police station, however bad the district might be. Things were worst in the City. Rent for one room in 1861 was 3s 7d (about 18p) a week. Many constables lived with their wives and several children in one such room, often in a filthy slum. In 1853 Commissioner Harvey gave the weekly budget for one of his constables, P. C. Andrews:

	£	s	d	
Wages	1	1	—	(£1.05)
Rent		4	6	
Bread		5	0	
Flour		1	0	
Tea		1	0	
Sugar			8	
Other food (no meat)		3	11	
Wood, coal, candles		1	8	
School fees			4	

Andrews was eventually left with about 3s 4d (17p) to pay for meat, clothing or medicine for himself, his wife and five children.

Pensions

Overwork, bad housing and too little food all combined to weaken many policemen until they were unfit for duty. They had a right to be considered for a pension, but in early days the amount a man received was left to the Commissioner. Harvey, the City Commissioner, would stop a man's pension if his conduct had not been good, even though the man was penniless and had served for ten or twenty years. He used this threat to keep discipline. Very few men survived long enough to draw a pension, compared to those who left, were dismissed, or died on duty.

After 1862 the Metropolitan Police paid a pension to a man who had served for fifteen years (increased if he had served longer) but it was not until 1890 that a policeman had a right to his pension, unless he had been dismissed for bad conduct. Sometimes a collection was made for a man who had been hurt on duty.

Police pensions were poor until near the end of the century. Nevertheless very few working men had any chance of a pension and had only the workhouse to look forward to, if they had not been able to save for their old age. It is important to compare police conditions with those of other trades *in the nineteenth century*, rather than today. By that standard the police were about as well off as the average manual worker. Nearer the end of the century the police did better than most workers.

Discipline

The police were highly disciplined. At the very beginning Rowan and Mayne threw out anyone who proved unsuitable for the 'new police', including a few criminals who had joined thinking that the uniform would enable them to get at valuable property more easily. Policemen were dismissed if a member of the public complained about them or, of course, if they committed any criminal act, or kept bad company, or broke police rules, such as being late on parade, improperly dressed, or leaving a beat.

The main cause of dismissal, or of the other penalty of being fined out of pay, seems to have been drunkenness. Unless they were members of the temperance movement, working people in the nineteenth century often drank hard. The reasons for this were many: pubs open all day, no pure drinking water, long hard hours of work with little time for relaxation, no social center except the pub. Policemen came from homes where beer-drinking at least was normal. From the first, however, the London police were not allowed to drink on

Scene in a London 'gin palace'. An off-duty policeman found here would be dismissed! This 1852 engraving by T. B. Smithies for The Workingman's Friend *was designed to show the horrors of drink. There are plenty of people waiting to take advantage of the drunks.*

duty. A sergeant's main job was to see that no one came on parade drunk. Sir Richard Mayne once dismissed an inspector with twenty-eight years' service, as well as sixty men at one time, for drinking at Christmas against his order.

The magazine *Punch* printed a little poem in 1845, which tells us what used to happen.

'Policeman to booze is gone, no watch patrols the lea.
The house that yonder stands alone invites to burglary.
The foot-pad prowls the heath and fen, no crusher stays his way.
Uprouse ye, then, my merry men, for now's your time of day.'

Later on in the nineteenth century life became a little easier for everyone, including the police. Drunkenness was less of a menace. In 1879 the Commissioner said:

'The offence of drunkenness is less severely dealt with than it used to be, and the decrease in the number of offences shows that the leniency of punishment has not operated badly...
the decrease is more due to the men being better looked after, and to their having had more means of recreation than they formerly had.'

Even so the police were under much stricter control than other working men, and this annoyed many of them. There were attempts to start a trade union for policemen in 1862. Men involved in this were dismissed and imprisoned. In 1890 some police went on strike in support of a bill to give them proper pensions. They also wanted to be able to form a union. They were dismissed. It was not until after the First World War that the Police Federation was formed.

Part of the reason why the government did not like the idea of a union was a fear that revolutionaries might take over the police. The police were to be kept out of politics, and policemen were not even allowed to vote in Parliamentary elections until 1887.

Policemen at work

A police constable was required to be on parade about fifteen minutes before he went on his beat. During this unpaid over-time his sergeant inspected him to see that he was sober and properly dressed, especially that he was not wearing his own boots or shoes. The sergeant read the police daily orders. The constable was supposed to remember or slowly write down names of wanted men, missing persons, places where robberies had been done and any special instructions. Then at about 6 p.m., if he was 'on nights' as most policemen were, he began the long march of his beat. The sergeant prepared to go out on inspection. The inspector remained in the station, dealing with prisoners or other routine work. Every so often the Superintendent himself might visit the station, the rattle of his horse and trap alerting everyone there.

Outside in the darkness the policeman would be 'shaking hands with doorknobs' or placing lengths of cotton across doors so that he could see if anyone had gone through when he returned to the spot. On most nights, nothing would happen at all. Pounding a beat was not at all lively and exciting.

Even a gin palace was better than the street. These people may not look very criminal, but the police are patrolling in threes in this district. This picture of a night patrol is by the famous French artist Gustave Doré, who published in 1871 a book based on sketches he had made during the previous four years.

Inspector Cavanagh recalled what it was really like after one o'clock in the morning:

'The streets belong to the police. A solitary wayfarer going home, or to work of some kind was all that was met with; and nothing disturbed the stillness of the night except the steady tramp of the policeman, or his customary "all right?" from the sergeant as he inspected his constables on the beat.'

Quite often the constables were more bothered about the sergeant and the inspector than about criminals. A policeman was in serious trouble if he was found to have left his beat, or was not at a certain place on the beat at the proper time. The result was that constables did not show much initiative. A former policeman wrote to the *Daily Telegraph* in 1865 that a police constable

'...gets tired and careless of his duties, and, instead of looking out for thieves, is dividing his time between glasses of ale, inspectors, drops of something "short" [spirits], sergeants, bits of cold mutton, and superintendents.'

The letter was written cheerfully, but there was plenty of truth in it. A policeman's best bet was to become friendly with servants in houses on his beat, so that they would give him a meal or a drink in the back kitchen. Pub keepers also found it a good idea to have an extra glass of beer within a passing policeman's reach. Snug alleyways and doors became known as quiet places to drain a drop of something or have a quick snack, heated on a little spirit stove such as some constables carried with them. This knowledge was handed on from constable to constable on a particular beat.

What happened to a constable on his beat depended mainly on which area of London he was patrolling. The suburbs which grew up over the nineteenth century were quiet and respectable. The constable's job was to prevent burglaries. We can see this by looking at the orders read to all the men in the Uniformed Branch of the Metropolitan Police on a perfectly ordinary day, 18 October 1877. There was some good news for 'X' Division, which had captured a burglar:

'This is a very good capture and reflects credit on the Police especially P.C. 116 Sims. Report result before Magistrate. Breaking into a warehouse—a good arrest, but it is very desirable to trace the property and other felons; as at present the balance is in favour of the thieves, two out of three being escaped with the property.'

'Burglaries at Sunbury. The apprehension of the thief is very satisfactory. Leave may be resumed in the section...'

Stopping police rest days if criminals were becoming a real menace in any division was often done. This provided extra men and sharpened up the policeman who lost his one day off each week. There had been less success in 'V' Division, in spite of the fact that it had had extra help:

'The Divisional Detectives of 'E' Division, specially employed to patrol, to appear here tomorrow, to answer for their remissness. The Superintendent of 'V' Division to attend also with witnesses, if any.'

In the central divisions life was often more exciting. White-chapel and the East End were notorious for violence, robberies and brawls. The criminal areas ('rookeries') were all close to the East End and the City. We shall look at them a little later. An important job was superintending common lodging houses. The police often looked for criminals here, and saw that there was some order kept. All kinds of casual thefts had to be followed up, and in the West End a constable spent much of his time keeping traffic and prostitutes moving along. The police also supervised theatres and music halls.

Policemen were quite often hurt in these areas, which were usually patrolled by two men. Murder was very rare, however. The first London policeman to be killed on duty was P.C. Grantham, who was kicked to death by Irish brawlers in Somers Town, near Euston, on 29 June 1830. The murderers escaped.

When his ten- or twelve-hour, twenty-mile walk was finished, a constable paraded once more at the police station. Then he was free, unless he had to go to court with any prisoners he had captured during the night, or to give evidence in another case.

Meanwhile the sergeant would be checking off his men, and finishing his own twelve-hour shift. The inspector on duty that morning would take over, and be ready to receive the police orders and messages, brought round by hand. The day constables would come on, ready to work a split shift in early morning and later afternoon. The Superintendent would be riding into Scotland Yard itself for the daily conference with the Commissioner.

At headquarters the Commissioner himself would be dealing with a stream of policemen charged with disciplinary offences, hearing evidence and giving judgement. Then he would review major crimes and deal with the vast number of letters containing complaints, requests and information which came to him every day.

The police commissioners worked every bit as hard as their

above: *The working poor of London had few chances of pleasure, but there might be a meal and some drink in 'The Kitchen' (this was in Gray's Inn Lane) or fun at the music hall (below). If the show was no good then the policeman on duty was another attraction. The drawing, also by Doré, shows a riot at the Garrick Theatre.*

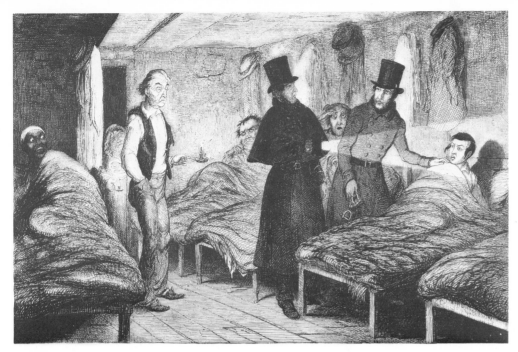

The end of the line. A robber is arrested in a cheap lodging house. The police kept a close watch on lodging houses, whose landlords often informed. From George Cruikshank, The Drunkard's Children, *1848.*

men, even though they had a small staff of clerks and lawyers to help. Mayne was famous for the long hours he kept. Finally the Commissioner might go to the Home Office in Whitehall to see the Home Secretary himself. Here he would discuss the biggest crimes, or any danger to the country which the police might have to deal with.

Twenty-four hours a day, every day of the year, the Uniformed Branch carried on its work. But was it really useful, and how did the police get on with the people they served?

The police and the people

Peel and the Commissioners left no doubt about how a policeman was to behave to those he met. Police orders told him that he was not to act as if he was a soldier in some army of occupation, but to enforce the law calmly and politely. Unfortunately no one had issued orders about how the people were to behave towards the police. The idea of law and order being enforced all the time was quite new to Londoners. Criminals knew they might be sought out by the Bow Street Runners, or overpowered and arrested by a watchman or a member of the Horse or Foot Patrols or the River Police. But all these people were about only at certain times and in certain places, and were easy to dodge. The arm of the law had never before been long enough to reach into parts of Clerkenwell and Houndsditch. In the past, a boy could expect to be over a wall and away before a watchman could catch him. Now he had to reckon with a policeman hearing his colleague's rattle, sounding the alarm and coming to help.

Those who were not criminal but just liked being independent objected to the police. Vegetable peddlers and other traders fought a kind of war of independence with the 'crushers'. Aristocrats, who disliked the idea that working people could now tell *them* what to do, used to pick fights with policemen and, if they could, would use their rank to avoid being punished. Drunken soldiers fighting their way back to barracks, rich man, poor man, beggarman, thief, each had his own quarrel with the police.

The people of London called the police by various nicknames: 'peeler', 'bobby', 'crusher' and, in Cockney back-slang, 'esclop'. The older 'raw lobster' went out with swallow-tail coats.

Yet the police did slowly win Londoners over. This was due above all to Peel's good sense. He had put the police in blue uniforms, not in the red of a soldier. He had kept their truncheons in pockets, out of sight, and their cutlasses in the police station. He had given very strict orders about conduct, and the Commissioners had enforced them.

Another reason why the police gradually became more popular was that the work they did was seen to be useful. As well as preventing crime and upholding the law, they developed the 'welfare' side of police work.

A policeman is often the first and only person 'in authority' who is on the scene when anything needs to be done. Therefore if a husband was thrashing his wife, or someone became ill, or mad, or a child was lost, then the policeman was expected to do something. People began to turn to the police for help, especially as social workers had not been thought of and in the slums clergy were few and far between. This built up a trust between the policeman and those on his beat. They might not like him, but they could see he was useful.

One part of police work was dealing with the poor and destitute. Sometimes wanderers and penniless immigrants were given a hard time, moved on, out of what little shelter they could find into the winter cold. Mainly the police tried to do what they could. Sometimes we can read between the lines of a policeman's report, and see that he was as angry as we would be over the cruelties of Victorian London. We could read many reports such as this one from the City of London Police, shortened from a report of 26 February 1842:

'Sarah Smith, 38, no home and her three children, completely destitute, found by P.C. 646 John Staples, on the step of the door No. 20 Wormwood Street. The Woman and her Children natives of London. Sent to the Relieving Officer, refused by Mr. Roberts any relief, on the ground that they had been found *one door* out of his union. Sent to the Relieving Officer, Seething Lane who gave an order for Stepney Green Workhouse.'

In choosing to recruit policemen from the ordinary people, and keeping them under strict discipline, yet making it clear that they were civilians in uniform, not soldiers, Sir Robert Peel had made the Metropolitan Police acceptable to Londoners. Other cities and counties followed London's example and set up their own police force.

The police were expected to help with the welfare of the poor. Destitute people had to get tickets from a police station before they received poor-relief. Why were the police used in this way? Picture from the Illustrated Times *of 1867.*

Did the police reduce crime?

The uniformed policeman may have become more popular between 1829 and 1900, but was he really efficient? This is a hard question to answer. We have figures of crimes known to the police, and numbers of arrests and convictions, and it looks as if numbers of crimes known went down as the nineteenth century went on. Unfortunately that does not prove that the police were becoming more efficient, because other causes could have brought the numbers of crimes and criminals down over the years. People were becoming less poor and desperate. There might have been fewer crimes even if the police force had never been set up. We do not know if people became more 'crime-conscious', and reported matters to the police in 1900 that would have been ignored if they had taken place in 1820, or 1850, or 1880.

The police themselves said they thought crime had diminished over the years, due to their efforts, but there could be other causes. We know of two famous events which did not reflect much credit on the police, and make us wonder how efficient they were.

The first of these was an outbreak in the 1860s of what was called garrotting, that is taking someone from behind and choking him with your arm. The garrotters were after money, of course, and worked in twos and threes. These attacks on innocent people by unknown and deadly thugs frightened Londoners, who demanded police action. The courts sentenced to heavy imprisonment the very few people arrested for violence, and Parliament brought back flogging for garrotters. It may have been a combination of strong police patrols and strict laws which caused garrotting to fade away, but we cannot be sure.

An even more famous case is that of Jack the Ripper. In 1888 at least five prostitutes were savagely murdered in Whitechapel. The way in which they were murdered was so horrible that every newspaper carried reports and all London knew the graphic details, even to the words of the constable who found the first victim so soon after she had been killed that, as he said, she was 'as warm as a toasted crumpet'. The police tried every method they could think of. Over six hundred plain-clothes men, as well as uniformed police, patrolled every inch of Whitechapel, and yet the Ripper could not be caught. Sir Charles Warren, the Commissioner, collected two bloodhounds (named Barnaby and Burgho) and tried to train them to follow scent in Hyde Park. The experiment ended when the bloodhounds set off at top speed – for bloodhounds – after the Commissioner himself! The murders did stop quite suddenly, and it is thought nowadays that the murderer may have been a lawyer who at the time was a schoolmaster in Blackheath, on the other side of the river. The police knew this man, who drowned himself in the Thames after the fifth, and last, murder.

Everyone, including Queen Victoria, was furious and blamed the police for not catching the Ripper.

It is clear from these and other cases that the police were not perfect, and that some of them do not seem to have been any use at all. Yet this does not mean that a patrolling force

An artist's impression of the discovery of Mary Nicholls's body in Whitechapel, 1888. This picture, and the picture on page 26, is from the Penny Illustrated Paper.

was a waste of money. We cannot know how many crimes were prevented by the approach of a policeman, and we should not forget the enormous difficulty of identifying and catching a totally unknown evildoer in a large town with a partly shifting population. For instance, in 1975 the Cambridge police had to catch a man who had raped eight women in the town. They used methods quite like those of the London police nearly ninety years before. They flooded the town with men. Superintendents themselves went back on the beat to help. A man was caught, but it took many weeks, even though the police had a description of their suspect and all the technological aids of the late twentieth century.

Barnaby and Burgho being trained, 1888. Although this idea did not work, police dogs have since been frequently used to catch criminals and to sniff out explosives and drugs.

It looks as if the biggest reason why the police were not more efficient was high 'turnover'; that is, the large numbers of men who left the force every year. Many had no choice – they were dismissed – but the hard working conditions caused large numbers to resign. Only 136 out of 1,815 men who had joined the City force in 1839 were still there ten years later. The Metropolitan force lost about five-sixths of its original numbers by 1833. About one man in five resigned after one or two years' service, some stayed a good deal less. It was difficult to build up a really expert force, even though there was no shortage of willing recruits.

The average police constable had very little education. It was enough that he could read and write, and do very simple arithmetic. The examination for Superintendent could be passed by anyone with a basic education who knew the details of the job. As we shall see, detectives were often little wiser. This meant that very few police officers had the education to cope with major enquiries and new developments in crime. The Commissioners, who were men of education, were also overworked and did not have the *practical* experience which serving police built up.

There are good reasons for thinking that the police could have been more efficient than they were. Even so, the uniformed peelers did their job. The force was designed to be cheap and simple, to get men out on the beat where they could see, and be seen, to keep order. They were to prevent crime. We can never know how many innocent people were *not* robbed or beaten up, because the sound of heavy boots came slowly up a dark alley, or a pickpocket did not see who was behind him.

5 Detectives

If a uniformed policeman was quick enough he might catch a criminal in the act. If he stood in the right place at the right time he might stop a crime being committed. This was not enough. There had to be ways of getting information in advance, so as to prevent crime, and of identifying and bringing to justice those who had actually broken the law.

An obvious method was to put some policemen into their ordinary clothes, where they could mix with any crowd and not be recognized. The difficulty in the early years was that some Londoners thought that even *uniformed* police were dangerous to freedom. Although the old Bow Street magistrates' office had had plain-clothes detectives until they were abolished in 1839, and some of these men continued to work with the police force, the idea of such 'spies' was very unpopular.

Divisional Detectives

After ten years or so, the police were trusted more and it was possible to use non-uniformed policemen more freely. In 1840 each division was ordered to choose an 'active, intelligent man' for tracing stolen property. This worked well and the system was continued. Instead of a uniform and a beat, some constables and sergeants wore their own clothes and had the job of solving particular cases as they came along. The job of tracing property was soon enlarged to tracing those who had stolen property. The police on that job were called Divisional Detectives. They usually worked on cases in their own divisional area. One Divisional Detective who had a specially interesting job later in the century was Sergeant Stammers, of 'A' Division. His Superintendent reported to the Commissioner in 1877 that

'He is engaged on making enquiries respecting larcenies, patrols and keeps a general supervision on all suspected persons frequenting the Division, from which sources several important apprehensions have been made.'

Stammers made 101 arrests in eight years and

'several of these he has apprehended in the Committee Rooms, House of Parliament, where constables in uniform have been on duty, they being unable to discover the perpetrators.'

Stammers had also rid Westminster Abbey of pickpockets (which earned him a reward from the Dean) and caught thieves on the new omnibuses. The report shows how valuable a plain-clothes man could be.

William Frith (1819–1909) painted many very accurate scenes of English life. The two detectives are looking very pleased at catching their man just as he is about to board the train at Paddington.

Divisional Detectives were required to get as much local information as they could. Another Superintendent explained one way in which they did this.

'When the inhabitants—particularly the shopkeeping class— see them about they take them into their confidence, sometimes for prudential reasons but at all times from kindly interest combined with curiosity in their really interesting pursuit.'

The detective was seen by some as 'glamorous' from the early days.

A detective used to drop in at beer-shops or 'servants' lurks', where dishonest servants would sometimes sell information about valuables in their houses to thieves. Old 'lags', who had just come out of prison, would earn a few shillings by passing on what they had learned inside. Gradually each detective would get to know where 'fences' lived, which lodging houses were safe and honest and which were dens of thieves, or very occasionally where a gang of forgers or coiners was operating. Most useful of all, he would quickly spot the appearance or disappearance of a famous face, always a good clue to crime.

Divisional Detectives were quite useful but it was clear that a force which could operate all over London, or outside the city altogether, was needed. In describing that force we can also explain one of the most famous names in Britain.

Scotland Yard

The headquarters of the Metropolitan Police in 1829 was a house, No. 4 Whitehall Place. Rowan and Mayne, the Commissioners, and a handful of senior officers and clerks worked there. The police station for 'A' (Whitehall) Division was newly built at the back of the house. It had its own entrance into a small square named Great Scotland Yard because it was supposed to have been an area where, centuries earlier, the ambassadors of the kingdom of Scotland had lodged.

The new detectives for the whole of London were stationed in part of the Scotland Yard and Whitehall Place buildings, and the name 'Scotland Yard' gradually attached itself to the detectives, and then to the whole headquarters. It may have been used earlier than 1842 when the eight policemen (six sergeants, two inspectors) began their work as detectives, though after-

Scotland Yard, the original headquarters of the Metropolitan Police. A constable is standing guard at one corner of the building.

wards 'the man from Scotland Yard' who appeared in the crime stories always meant a detective.

The Detective Branch was nothing like the vast modern detective system. By 1864 there were only fifteen men, including the clerks, at Scotland Yard. Even as late as 1886 there was still a cosy sort of atmosphere. Detective Inspector Lansdowne remembered it as it was at that time. The senior inspectors had 'the large front room on the right', with Superintendent Shore in his office behind; 'the clerks in a little den close by'. Superintendent Adolphus ('Dolly') Williamson, who grew roses on his few days off, was next to the Assistant Commissioner. 'Above them on the second floor were other Inspectors and...the correspondence department.' The lowly detective sergeants lived in the basement. If Sherlock Holmes had been a real person he and Watson would have taken a hansom cab from 221 B Baker Street, through Mayfair perhaps, along Piccadilly, down Whitehall and turned left into Whitehall Place, to meet the best detectives in Britain.

The Scotland Yard men were handpicked from the most intelligent and successful uniformed constables and younger sergeants. Williamson, when a young constable, had spent his spare time learning French while his friends were at the music hall, or taking it easy in the section house. At the end of the century Percy Savage, the son of a policeman, learned shorthand and technical drawing, on his father's advice. G. W. Cornish spent his spare time 'doing unofficial detective work in various places where useful information could be found'. Both men rose to be Superintendents. Detectives needed skills which the ordinary policeman did not. Lansdowne was chosen because he had done well, and was lucky enough to be noticed;

'in two or three cases, one of highway robbery and another of housebreaking, I had caught the men; and otherwise I had rendered Mr. Williamson assistance in regard to burglaries. I was therefore sent to the "Yard" and became a detective sergeant and subsequently inspector.'

The detective's trade

Detectives need patience, persistence, courage and cunning. A favourite trick was to disguise oneself as an innocent tradesman or country boy and get to know a suspected man or his friends. That required a knowledge of trades, and sometimes regional accents as well. Setting up a trap – such as sending a parcel via a post office to a suspect who collected his mail there, and catching him when he arrived – was another ruse a detective had to learn. Foreign languages, knowledge of foreigners and the ability to live for a while in a foreign country all counted in a detective's favour.

One kind of 'foreign' language every detective had to know was thieves' slang. This was almost a proper language in itself. It was sometimes called 'cant'. Criminals of every country still have slang words they use amongst themselves which sometimes become known through films or novels. In Victorian times, and for centuries before, criminals had lived among the very poor in town and country. Since children of criminal families rarely went to school or had much to do with 'respectable' people, they learned the language more deeply than children learn slang today. Cant came partly from Romany, the language of the gypsies (who were travelling people, but by no means all criminal), from English regional dialects and slang,

from Irish, and from some very old London words, which went back to the poor and the criminals of the Middle Ages. Some of these were known in Shakespeare's time. A very few are still in use today; Londoners at least might understand such words as 'duds', 'flash', 'chiv', 'lag', 'topped', 'doss'. Cockney rhyming slang and back slang ('yob', 'esclop', 'eno', 'owt', 'erth') was also used by criminals as well as vegetable peddlers, because it prevented outsiders from knowing what was being said. The words changed as the old links with the countryside faded out, and new groups of immigrants came to the city, bringing their slang with them—'gonif', 'schemozzle', 'scarper'. But a Scotland Yard man in a lodging house who did not know what to answer when his drinking partner asked 'Voker Romeny?' would never learn a thing about criminals, because any real travelling man would recognize at least that he was being asked if he knew gypsy language.

A detective often worked alone. This meant that he sometimes risked his life. Lansdowne once went in a hansome cab with a suspected man to check an alibi. When it proved that the man's story was a lie, he broke down and confessed. He had forged a cheque. Lansdowne took him back in the cab, keeping his hand on the tail of the man's long coat. Suddenly his suspect whipped round with a revolver in his hand: '"Let me go or you are a dead man!" He did not wait but pulled the trigger. I heard the hammer fall with a click but there was no explosion.' Lansdowne went for the gun. A crowd gathered. In 1829 they might have freed the criminal, but now about fifty years later, the people's feelings were the other way about. A big coalman saw his chance and grabbed the man from behind while Lansdowne tore the revolver from his grip. Back went detective and prisoner in the hansom cab. The revolver had five bullets and one empty chamber.

In the rookeries

Detectives operated all over London, mainly alone, sometimes with the Uniformed Branch. In some areas the detectives became as well known as any 'beat' policeman. They knew criminals more closely than any other police, and they knew the areas where criminals lived.

Although most of the poorer districts of London sheltered some criminals, some areas were almost entirely criminal and near-criminal. These were known as 'rookeries'. No honest man or woman, except for a few bold writers, and, later in the century, men such as Dr Barnardo, ever went into them. Rookeries were not very big; their strength lay in being disorderly. A good description of the famous St Giles rookery was given by W. A. Miles in 1839.

'The nucleus of crime in St. Giles's consists of about six streets, riddled with courts, alleys, passages and dark entries, all leading to rooms and smaller tenements...There is, moreover, an open communication at the backs of all the houses, so that directly a panic is created, men and women and boys may be seen scrambling in all directions through the back yards and over the party walls, to effect an escape... the lowest grade of thieves and dissolute people live in the **immediate neighbourhood of the station house [police station], near George St., formerly Dyott St....** at least one-third of the London beggars live in St. Giles's...The clerk of this Division of the Police thinks every publican, except two, in St. Giles's are fences.'

In the early part of the nineteenth century it was impossible for anyone to catch a criminal, once he was safe in the rookery. He might be betrayed and lured out by his 'friends', but that was a different matter. By 1840 things were beginning to change.

In November of that year the police were tipped-off that a gang of coiners had set up a 'factory' in a room in the middle of St Giles. Coiners were always difficult to convict, because if they had advance warning of the police, they tipped all the evidence into the furnace used to melt the metal. A surprise attack was necessary. The coiner's house faced onto a narrow street. At least six armed policemen in plain clothes quietly assembled. They burst into the house and caught the coiners with all their equipment.

Then came the real problem. As soon as the handcuffed men were seen leaving the house up went a cry 'Rescue! Rescue!' A mob gathered and began to stone the police. Down some of them went.

At that moment a squad of uniformed police who had been waiting outside the rookery smashed their way through the mob and began to drag the prisoners towards Bloomsbury Square. Although there was a police station only a hundred yards away it lay further *inside* the rookery, and there was no chance of getting there. Reinforcements waited with cabs. Inch by inch the police fought their way to the square. There was a final rush; one man tried to stab the inspector just as he rushed across the square to a cab, dragging his handcuffed prisoner. The police moved off as quickly as they could. The mob retreated furiously into its fortress once again.

About ten years later Charles Dickens, the novelist, who was very interested in everything concerned with London, especially police and criminals, visited some rookeries with the famous Detective Inspector Field. (Field retired in 1852, aged forty-seven.)

First they met P.C. Rogers who went with them to the St Giles lodging houses which were on his beat, and then to the most savage rookery still remaining, near Petticoat Lane (the popular name for Middlesex Street). Two men were set to guard the door, and the party went into the basement, full of thieves, who watched, silently, hatred on every face.

'The Devil's Acre', by Doré. Consider how difficult it would be to catch someone among the nest of houses.

Women waiting for their husbands to come out of the pub, to try and 'rescue' some housekeeping money. The policeman also waits, by the lamp post in the background. The picture appeared in 'The trial of Sir Jasper', a poem of the 1870s against alcoholism.

The man who owned the house, a fence called Bark, even thought that the police could be attacked. He tried to persuade the others. Dickens tells the story in his own style:

"'If the adjective coves in the kitchen was men they'd come up now and do for you...They'd come up and do for you"

cries Bark again, and waits. We are shut up, half-a-dozen of us, in Bark's house in the innermost recesses of the worst part of London and in the dead of night – the house is crammed with notorious robbers and ruffians – and not a man stirs. No, Bark. They know the weight of the law and they know Inspector Field and Co. too well.'

Indeed they did know Field. He could have them transported to Australia. Dickens describes him visiting a lodging house:

'Inspector Field is the bustling speaker. Inspector Field's eye is the roving eye that searches every corner of the cellar as he talks. Inspector Field's hand is the well-known hand that has collared half the people here, and motioned their brothers, sisters, fathers, mothers, male and female friends inexorably to New South Wales...in the rear Detective Sergeant plants himself, composedly whistling, with his right arm across the narrow passage.'

Charles Dickens (and Inspector Field) both liked telling a dramatic story, and perhaps Dickens laid on the villainy a little, but Dickens was a genuine expert on London life and police work. His account shows that it still needed a strong force of police, possibly armed, to penetrate the worst rookeries and come out unharmed. Yet Inspector Field was obviously safer than the other police had been only a few years before. P.C. Rogers patrolled the St Giles area every night.

The police were getting the rookeries under control as the nineteenth century went on. They were helped by two things. London was settling down after about 1850, the slums becoming *slowly* less filthy and savage. The gradual growth of law and order made the free criminal life of the rookery very difficult. Secondly and more important, London needed big new roads to cope with all the trade coming through the docks and around the city. These roads were sometimes deliberately planned to go through rookeries and open them up. New Oxford Street (1842) did just that for St Giles, and though the district remained 'rough' it was never again a thieves' fortress.

The same is true of other rookeries. Field Lane and Saffron Hill were reduced by cutting Charterhouse Street and Farringdon Street. In the same way Commercial Street broke open the Whitechapel rookery in the 1850s. More criminals moved in none the less, as those who found life too difficult shifted to Seven Dials or Limehouse. Whitechapel had always been a district full of thieves since the beginning of the nineteenth century, and was to stay that way until the 1900s. Near the end of the century the population changed once more, as many Jews from Eastern Europe settled there.

Dirty work at the Yard

Although everyone seems to have heard of Scotland Yard, and there has always been some glamour about being a detective (as the popularity of detective stories in films, books and television shows), the work itself has always been hard, and sometimes unpleasant.

Every day the Superintendent of each Metropolitan Police division sent in a crime report to headquarters. If a Scotland Yard man was needed then off he had to go, straight away. Police forces outside London called on Scotland Yard to 'lend' them an expert detective to tackle a really serious robbery, or a murder. Detectives quite often went abroad to trace wanted men, or deal with international crime, such as fraud.

Detectives had to get results. They had to work at all sorts of times, in all sorts of places, often with no help near, and were blamed if they failed in their special tasks. For these reasons many uniformed policemen did not want to become detectives. This meant that some of the Divisional Detectives were not as good as they were supposed to be. Some uniformed men were even put into plain clothes because they always looked scruffy in uniform, which hardly suggests that they were the pride of the force. When it was suggested (in 1871) that each detective should keep a daily working diary, Superintendent Williamson had to tell the Commissioners that 'a number of them who are employed as divisional detectives would from want of education find it impossible to make a daily comprehensive report of their proceedings; this would keep out of the detective service many useful men'.

The uniformed policemen did not always get on well with detectives. They envied the freedom of action a detective had, but they sometimes thought that mixing with criminals rubbed onto the detectives themselves. In 1880 Williamson wrote a confidential note to the Commissioner about the problems of recruiting good men. He wrote about

'the uncertainty and irregularity of the duties, which are also in many cases very distasteful and repugnant to the better class of men in the service as their duties constantly bring

left: *Superintendent Adolphus Williamson, a Victorian detective.*

right: *Kate Hamilton's was one of the most famous Victorian 'night houses'. Kate is at the back, keeping an eye on the customers. From Henry Mayhew,* London Labour and the London Poor, *c. 1860.*

far right: *Sir C. E. Howard Vincent (1849–1908), founder of the C.I.D. and its Director from 1878 to 1884. He was afterwards a Conservative politician.*

them into contact with the lowest classes, frequently with much unnecessary drinking, and compels them at all times to resort to tricky practices, which they dislike'.

Spies again. Williamson knew about 'tricky practices' because he used money to pay informers. In May 1875 he was allowed to use £20 to try to find out more about some jewel thieves. And £20 was about four months' pay for a senior police constable at this time.

Sadly, it was not only criminals who were prepared to take bribes. In 1877 Williamson had a puzzling case. A gang was making huge profits by running a betting swindle. One woman had lost £30,000. Detectives were going all over Britain and abroad and yet there were no important arrests. The truth came out when one unimportant member of the gang was picked up at last. Williamson's own men were being bribed by the gang to give them information about police plans. Into prison went Inspector Meiklejohn, Inspector Druscovitch – a brilliant officer who could speak several languages – and others.

We do not know how corrupt Victorian policemen were. No doubt detectives and men on the beat had their 'perks': free meals here and there, or a birthday present from someone besides their Mum, but there were very few serious cases of corruption proved against the London police.

The biggest temptations in the nineteenth century came from 'night houses', that is, drinking and gambling clubs where prostitutes were picked up. Some of these were shabby and dangerous, others luxurious places which catered to the rich and famous. Police in the West End were worth bribing if they would warn that a raid was coming, or look the other way when they heard tales about a particular place. Sir Henry Smith, who was a senior policeman himself later on, said that under Sir Richard Mayne 'the whole 'C' Division was corrupt to the core'. He mentioned one 'night house' 'where a constable—whose salary, I imagine, must have exceeded the Home Secretary's—stood nightly at the door'.

In fact, a few years later, Mayne did find out about the corruption. A whole force of men, whose faces were not known, went on plain-clothes duty in the West End and tried to 'clean up' the area. No one was prosecuted. The police were always cautious about interfering with the 'upper classes'. They would bring any suspect to trial, whoever he was, if otherwise he would remain unpunished; but those who came of wealthy and respectable families were sometimes given the chance to go abroad for life, so as to avoid disgracing their families.

However, the detectives' case was not like that. It was a public scandal and action had to be taken to root out every dishonest man, and to re-establish the detective branch. A special committee of enquiry was set up, and reported to the Home Office that the Detective Department (which *Punch* magazine insisted on calling the 'Defective' Department) should be modernized.

Williamson was an honest man and a good detective, but old-fashioned. The Department was reorganized and given a new name, Criminal Investigation Department, now known by its initials. The new post of Director of Criminal Investigation was given to Howard Vincent, who had never been a policeman but had written a careful report on the French detective system, which helped to get him the job. Vincent ranked directly below the Commissioner himself.

Vincent tried a number of new ideas, including recruiting men directly into the Detective Branch without any service on the beat. The police have always disliked men coming in from 'outside' and Vincent's hand-picked men were not successful. He still expanded the detective force from about 250 (including Divisional Detectives) to about 800. This was not many for so vast a city as London.

New Scotland Yard. The famous building on the Thames Embankment was designed in the 'Victorian Gothic' style by Norman Shaw. Building was started around 1885. This picture, from The Graphic *of 1890, shows the building when it was first occupied, with the Houses of Parliament in the background.*

Modernizing the police

Vincent was also one of the few policemen who took a serious interest in scientific aids to detection. The nineteenth-century police were very slow to see how science could help them.

The electric telegraph was invented in 1844. In 1845 a clever policeman used the new Great Western Railway telegraph from Slough to Paddington to help catch a murderer who had escaped by train. Even so, it was not until after 1868 that telegraph wires linked up most police stations. The telephone was installed in New Scotland Yard when the police moved

there from Whitehall Place, in 1890, but only for use inside the building. As late as 1917 there were still two police stations in London not connected to the public exchange.

Messages were distributed by hand until late in the century. Superintendents went in person to Scotland Yard every morning.

The most important of all twentieth-century inventions to affect the police, the automobile, was taken up just as slowly. Superintendent Savage, who joined in 1901, said that there were no cars in use when he was a recruit, and the police generally were not issued with cars until 1918. The River Police

Two advances in police work. The cartoon on the left is from the humorous magazine Judy *of 1891.* right: *The River Police station at Waterloo pier. The use of first steam and then gasoline launches helped the police to protect the valuable cargoes and property on the Thames.*

steam launches were introduced only in 1885, and there were no reliable motor boats until after 1901.

The only new invention which the police took up pretty quickly was identification by finger-prints, and photographs. The latter were in use from before 1889, when the 'Rogues Gallery' was built up. Identifying those who were caught, let alone catching people from clues, was an enormous problem. Very few ordinary people carried documents that could identify them; they did not have passports or bank accounts; driving licences and credit cards were still far in the future.

Criminals gave as many false names as possible, and travelled over the country by rail, committing offences in many places. A man might be caught in one place and treated as a first offender, even though he had 'done time' for robberies elsewhere. A useful way of identifying a suspect was to ask a policeman who might have arrested him earlier if he recognized the man. Detectives would go to a prison specially to see men being released, and would try to memorize their appearance.

There were two quick ways of knowing if a man had been convicted. The first was the famous 'prison crop'. Convicts had their heads shaved. This only lasted for a short time after release, but the marks of a flogging in prison remained on a

man's back for life. If he was caught again the scars literally branded him as a criminal.

It is not surprising that when Galton and others showed that everyone has his own set of finger-prints, which are like no one else's, and which stay the same throughout life, then Scotland Yard became very interested.

The leading English expert was Edward Henry, who was Inspector-General of Police for Bengal. In 1901 he accepted the job of setting up a finger-print library for the Metropolitan Police, and from 1903 to 1918 he was Commissioner.

At first judges and juries could not believe that finger-prints at the scene of a crime could be certain evidence. After a time the value of finger-prints came to be understood, and many a man who left his 'dabs' on a table or a glass had time in his cell to be sorry about the mistake.

Science was coming to the aid of crime detection by the beginning of the twentieth century, without replacing the skill and knowledge of detectives, or the routine patrolling of the uniformed branch. Compared with a Bow Street Runner, and Inspector Field, a modern C.I.D. man still needs the same skills, and still faces many of the same conditions: long hours, low company, many temptations, and sometimes deadly danger.

6 The safety of the state

The Metropolitan Police have always had two jobs. One is preventing crime and catching criminals. The other is keeping the peace during mass demonstrations and large crowds, and restoring order if fights and riots break out. This job is every bit as hard as catching thieves.

It was given to the 'new police', indeed to the very same policemen who patrolled the streets every day. This is different from many other countries, which have two sorts of police: those used for 'ordinary' crime and traffic duties, and a body much more like soldiers, sometimes living apart in barracks, designed to fight and put down revolts, riots and violent demonstrations. The C.R.S. in France and the Guardia Civil in Spain are police forces of this kind, and the Royal Irish Constabulary was in some ways similar.

Peel also made the decision that the police should not carry firearms when dealing with crowds. This also stopped the police becoming 'men apart'. Peel's decision stood the test of time, and helped to make the police accepted eventually by almost all the public.

Riot and commotion

In 1829 the 'new police' were not accepted at all. They were an unknown quantity. Everyone was waiting to see if they were going to be used as a government 'army' to put down opposition.

The first big test came in 1833. A meeting of a body called the National Union of the Working Classes met at Cold Bath Fields, near Clerkenwell. A large force of police was assembled to keep order.

There are a good many versions of what happened. The police said they controlled the meeting with as little force as possible. Many of those at the meeting said the police attacked them without provocation. Certainly the police expected trouble; they were issued with their cutlasses, which were never carried on normal duties. Nevertheless it is true that no demonstrator died, although one policeman, P.C. Robert Culley, of 'C' (St James's) Division, was killed. The police were so much disliked at this time that the inquest jury gave a verdict of 'justifiable homicide'. The jurymen themselves were given a dinner in their honour and a medal each. An official inquiry cleared the police.

The police learned by long experience that the best way to keep a meeting or procession orderly was to plan carefully in advance, have a very large number of policemen on the spot, and keep those policemen under cool and strict discipline. Failure in any one of these respects might encourage violence, in which not only rioters but police and peaceful people might be hurt.

The highest officers of the police sometimes faced a mob direct. Sir Richard Mayne had been Commissioner for over thirty years when he had to deal with a riot in Hyde Park. The Home Secretary had forbidden a meeting of the Reform League (which wanted changes in voting for Parliament) to be held in the park. The park railings gave way under the pressure of people. Inspector Cavanagh described Mayne:

'The poor old fellow, sticking to his post in the most gallant manner and giving orders right and left, was struck in the face by some cowardly scoundrels by stones thrown at him, the blood streaming down his venerable face.'

The riot had been allowed to happen partly through Mayne's bad planning. He died in 1868, partly as a result of strain caused by failing to control riots.

London was a peaceful city, compared to many of those in Europe, and the police were not faced with major demonstrations again until the late 1880s. Then the growing number of unemployed, and the efforts of trade unions to become organized, caused much conflict. In 1886 a meeting of the London Working Men's Committee, in Trafalgar Square, was expected to lead to violence. The seventy-four year old Superintendent

RUFFIANLY POLICEMAN

ABOUT TO PERPETRATE A BRUTAL AND DASTARDLY ASSAULT ON THE PEOPLE.

above: *Pulling down railings so as to hold a meeting without permission in Hyde Park. It was in this riot that Commissioner Mayne was hurt. From the* Illustrated London News, *1866.*

above right: *A* Punch *cartoon replying to the usual accusations of 'police brutality' made after the 1866 riots.*

below: *Mr. Marsham, a magistrate, arrives to read the Riot Act in the Trafalgar Square riot of 1887. Note the mounted police as well as his escort of the Life Guards. From* The Graphic.

Walker was in charge. All that happened at the meeting itself was that Walker had his pocket picked. However, at the end of the afternoon a group of roughs in the crowd left the square by a route the police had not expected, and hundreds of people followed them. The crowd spent about an hour breaking the windows of clubs and shops, and looting. It took one inspector and sixteen men five minutes to disperse them – when they reached the crowd. Walker and his superior officers had made such a mess of the arrangements that there were no police anywhere in the area! The electric telegraph, which could have warned police stations all around, was not even used.

In November 1887 there were further demonstrations, some lasting more than one day, in which thousands of police and rioters fought very bitterly. Members of a group called the Social Democratic Federation wanted to meet in Trafalgar Square. Permission was refused, but large numbers of men marched on the square from every side. The army had been called out because the government feared that the police would not be able to control the riots. The Life Guards were given live ammunition and placed around the square, to guard public buildings. A magistrate was ready to read the Riot Act (which would have given troops the legal right to open fire if necessary and if the crowd did not disperse promptly). In fact the police were able to control the riot, with some help from the Guards, without anyone firing a shot. Nevertheless, two of the crowd died and many policemen were badly hurt.

At the inquiry afterwards it was found that Sir Charles Warren, the Commissioner, had not made proper plans. The police were too short of inspectors and superintendents when faced with such big demonstrations.

Sir Charles resigned in 1888, partly because of these riots, and because of his failure to catch Jack the Ripper.

The police had done one job well. There was no need for the army to fire on the crowd because the police were able to put the rioters down without bullets. Even so, it was clear that the police had not yet learned to keep demonstrations always peaceful.

The Fenians

The policeman's job was becoming a little easier in the 1870s than it had been in 1829, so far as ordinary crime was concerned. Yet it was in this period that the police had to deal with something quite new: trouble from outside London. The troubles of Ireland had spread to England.

During the nineteenth century – and later – some Irishmen believed that their country was being cruelly oppressed by the rest of Britain, and the only way to make it truly free and independent was by force. From time to time secret societies were formed, and plans made for campaigns of violence. The most important of these societies was the Irish Republican Brotherhood, usually called the Fenian Society, founded in 1858 by James Stephens and Thomas Luby. A Fenian rising in Ireland in 1867 failed and many of the leading members of the movement were sent to prison, some in England.

In December 1867 a secret service agent in Ireland warned the police that there was a plot to free two Fenians, Burke and Casey, imprisoned in Clerkenwell jail. The prison was to be blown up. Sir Richard Mayne, in his last year as Commissioner, did not take precautions. The police thought a bomb would be put under the prison, perhaps in a sewer. In fact the Fenians brought a bomb in a barrel on a little cart, put it against the wall and set it off. Four people were killed and many children playing in the street were badly hurt. Police nearby were knocked down by the force of the explosion. The prisoners did not get away because the prison authorities had changed the time when they were let out of their cells for exercise. Eventually one Fenian bomber, Barrett, was caught, and became the last man ever to be hanged in public in England.

In 1882–3 a combined force of Irish and English detectives helped to bring another group, called the 'Invincibles', to justice, after they had murdered the Chief Secretary for Ireland and his companion, in Phoenix Park, Dublin.

In 1883 the Special Irish Branch of the C.I.D. was set up. When the 'Troubles' in Ireland died down temporarily the word 'Irish' was dropped, but the name Special Branch remained for the part of the C.I.D. which dealt with plots against the state, especially political assassinations.

The Special Branch has remained the most confidential of all parts of the Metropolitan Police. Little has been written about what it did in the nineteenth century. Some of the evidence is in the Public Record Office but no one will be allowed to see it until after the year 2000. Even so, we do know some things about the Special Branch and those who worked in it, and one such man in particular, because he wrote his autobiography.

An early Special Branch detective

John Sweeney was born in 1857 in County Kerry, Ireland. He later moved to London with his family. He was too short for the Royal Irish Constabulary, whose smart uniform he liked, so he joined the Metropolitan Police instead. He was posted to 'T' (Hammersmith) Division. The local Inspector recognized that Sweeney was keen and intelligent. He made him a clerk for part of the seven years he was a constable. This gave him some experience of administration and police work in general. In 1884 Sweeney was promoted, and sent to Scotland Yard as a probationary detective. His main job was fighting the Fenians, who nearly killed him. In May 1884 Scotland Yard itself was blown up. Sweeney tells what happened to him:

'By a piece of extraordinary good fortune there was at the actual moment absolutely no one in our offices... I was busy making out a report, but on finishing it I also went out, thus escaping death... It was ascertained that the dynamite had been placed in a lavatory in the north-west corner of the building. We never discovered how the bomb was ignited...'

Sweeney's souvenir was a shattered desk and chair, where he had been working a few minutes before the bomb went off.

left: *Queen Victoria and the Prince of Wales meet Czar Nicholas II of Russia at Balmoral in 1896. From the* Illustrated London News.

far left: *A bomb at Scotland Yard, 1884. The blast would have damaged the policeman's hearing, which is why one hand has gone to his ear while the other fends off flying glass. This is a rather imaginative artist's impression from the* Illustrated London News.

Later, Sweeney served as a royal bodyguard. (This job is still carried out by the Special Branch.) He described the security precautions made when Queen Victoria visited Dublin in 1900:

'A conference every morning was held by the principal officers; and when the Queen's programme for the day was telephoned to us we distributed our watchful forces along the streets through which the Queen would pass. But we were not active only during her Majesty's actual movements. At night we visited certain inns and various other rendezvous where evil-designed persons might be met; nor did we neglect to keep the railway stations and quay under careful observation.'

Nothing happened to the Queen, which pleased Sweeney, who writes that he was proud to be both an Irishman and an English police officer.

The most dangerous times were during the visits of foreign rulers to England. Sweeney had to look after the Russian secret police who came to escort Czar Nicholas II in 1896. He did not enjoy it. They spoke no English and 'they did not lack the habitual reserve and caution of the police agent, especially the Russian variety of the type'. The Czar gave him some diamond and gold cufflinks, however.

Such gifts were welcome, even though they did not lighten the hard routine of watching and listening which is at the heart of all detective work. The Special Branch kept a close eye on anyone suspected of plotting. Such work put a greater strain on Special Branch men than any other variety of policeman. When Chief Inspector Littlechild described his work to an inquiry on police pensions in 1889, he spoke of twelve- to fourteen-hour working days. On one case he was writing and receiving seventy to eighty letters every day. Arresting suspects and giving evidence took up many hours. Reports had to be written at the end of a very long day. The constant watching was worst of all. Sometimes a detective would be twelve hours without food or shelter, afraid to take his eyes off a street door for a moment, in case he missed a wanted man. Littlechild had been blown up himself by a terrorist bomb, and though he was a successful officer, he had had enough. He was asked at the inquiry: 'You would rather like to get out of the special Department, if you could?' 'Yes, certainly, that is the fact; the ordinary crime department is far preferable to political conspiracy work'.

Once more it is clear that even in the Special Branch, a detective's life was hard, tough and exhausting, whatever impression stories about spies might give.

7 The Sidney Street siege

By the year 1910 the London police had over eighty years of experience behind them. The story of the 'Sidney Street siege' tells us much about what had changed in those eighty years (and what had not), as well as illustrating how London coped with what we now call 'terrorists'.

England before the First World War was more peaceful and stable than many European countries. There was a tradition of freedom which permitted those who had fallen out with the government of their own country to live in Britain. Provided they did not break British law they could do what they liked, and believe what they pleased. Many such refugees came and lived peaceful and harmless lives. One of those who arrived in 1849 was an almost unknown scholar from Germany, Karl Marx.

Some refugees took a different line, and the most dangerous of these were the anarchists. Anarchists believe that every sort of government is bad, and some anarchists believed that it was therefore a good thing to get rid of any and every ruler with bombs and bullets. That is why royal visits took up so much of Inspector Sweeney's time.

Murder in the City

Late in the evening of Friday, 16 December 1910, a trader in Houndsditch heard tunnelling noises coming from somewhere close to his house. The shop next door was a jeweller's, an obvious target. Max Weil was used to England and went in search of a policeman. Houndsditch was in the City and the first man he met was P.C. Piper, a probationary constable in the City of London force, on his beat. Piper listened, and went round to the street at the back of the jeweller's. He knocked at the house which seemed nearest. A man opened it but looked so suspicious that Piper pretended nothing much was wrong and went for reinforcements. The two constables patrolling nearby beats, plus a sergeant and two plain-clothes men in the

neighbourhood, were rounded up. A patrolling force provided plenty of men quickly, just as Peel had intended it should.

Police Sergeant Bentley knocked at the door. It was opened, Bentley went in. After a few seconds there was a blaze of a revolver, flashes and shots. A whole gang of people raced out of the house, firing as they came. The police tackled them, except for one man who took cover. There was a furious struggle, with the police going for their men even as they were

The murder of three London policemen in December 1910. This sketch from the Daily Graphic *is not accurate in detail but gives a vivid impression of the scene.*

being hit again and again by bullets. One member of the gang shot another by mistake, and at this they ran for the entrance to the street, dragging their wounded comrade with them, while injured and dying policemen were helped by the first people to come out of the surrounding houses.

Things were so confused that the gang managed to get away, and it was not until about midnight that Detective Superintendent Ottaway arrived with a group of armed policemen and began to interview witnesses. They had little more than unreliable descriptions from the few people who had seen the gang walking quickly away, with the wounded man being taken for a drunk.

The gang had gone to 59 Grove Street, off the Commercial Road, Stepney. They searched for a doctor for the dying man. When a doctor came he saw what had happened but did not tell the police until the following day.

When the doctor's telephone call came at last, Detective Inspector Frederick 'the Weasel' Wensley was told. Wensley had been stationed in Whitechapel for over twenty years. He knew the East End and its people inside out. Since he was in the Metropolitan Police he was put to work with Detective Inspector Thompson of the City Police. The two forces in London were working closely together.

The detectives hurried to Grove Street. They found the dead body of a man, surrounded by guns and ammunition, in a room full of anarchist literature and papers. As Sergeant Leeson rushed into the back room he found no one but a small hunch-backed woman, who was trying to burn a few of the papers. Amazingly, a man actually knocked at the door of the house while the police were there and asked for 'Fritz'. His name was Nicholas Tomacoff, and he had heard nothing about the murders. He, and the hunchbacked woman, whose name was Sara Trassjonsky, were taken to City Police headquarters in Old Jewry.

When the police studied the papers found at Grove Street they found that the dead man, who had been shot by a comrade escaping from the jeweller's, was called George Gardstein. He had a membership card for an anarchist–communist group in Latvia and other documents showed that he was closely in touch with other anarchists and revolutionaries all over Europe. Most of these letters were about providing money for other anarchists in the Czar of Russia's prisons. (Latvia was, and still is, under Russian rule.) Other letters explained how to make bombs. The City Police immediately contacted the Special Branch, because these were matters that affected the security of the state and lives of its leaders.

They explained also why the doctor who treated Gardstein took so long to telephone the police, and why witnesses were slow to come forward. Let us look at this for a moment.

Frightened people

Peel had set up the London police as a force of unarmed civilians in uniform, told always to be polite and friendly to ordinary citizens. The result was that honest people trusted them and were willing to come forward with information that would help them. Even criminals knew that the police were unarmed, and so they did not often carry guns themselves. Many of the people who lived in Whitechapel in 1910 were refugees from the Russian Empire. The majority were Jewish. They were poor people from the ghettos of Russia, the Baltic states and Poland. *Their* experience of authority had been the lash and the gun. The Russian police were brutal, especially when dealing with Jews. They kept 'law and order' by from time to time stirring up 'pogroms', when Jews were robbed, beaten and killed indiscriminately. Police were hated, and those who fought against them were themselves as savage as the police. That was why Gardstein and the others never thought twice about shooting their way out of Houndsditch. The people of the area spoke Yiddish, Russian, Latvian, not English. They did not understand English ways and their main wish was to avoid any contact with authority. Even when shopkeepers and stallholders were victims of protection rackets, or wrecked by rival gangs of immigrants (Bessarabians and Odessians for example) fighting forty at a time, they would not go to the police. Many of them could not understand why the English police had not begun a pogrom in the district, immediately after the shooting. If they had known that the doctor had told the police he had treated Gardstein, then they would have boycotted him.

The anarchists who killed Sergeant Bentley and two other police on the night of 16 December lived in an even more alien world than other immigrants. They looked only for the revolution, especially in Russia. England was a place to get money and live while plotting. Cheap rooms, anarchist clubs, coded letters, travel, a risky dash back to Latvia; this was their life.

left: *Jewish immigrants just landed in London, 1902. These people probably came from Russia or Poland. All they own is in their bags and baskets.*

below: *Jewish tailors in the East End of London.*

The police therefore had two jobs. The first was to catch those who had murdered their comrades. But these were not ordinary criminals; they were anarchists. Was there a plot to murder the King or the Prime Minister? Special Branch needed to know much more about the whole network of anarchists and other revolutionaries in London.

Tomacoff, the man who had come to 59 Grove Street and asked for 'Fritz', was a Russian musician, who had played at the anarchist club. The man he had come to see was called Fritz Svaars. Although only in his mid-twenties Svaars had already been arrested in Riga (on suspicion of killing a policeman) and had twice escaped. He was one of the Houndsditch murderers, though the police did not know this at first. Tomacoff gave a list of all the friends and acquaintances he had met when he had visited Svaars. One of these was the woman found in Gardstein's room, Sara Trassjonsky.

Searching

The police went to see everyone they could on Tomacoff's list. Wensley and his tough assistant Sergeant Bert Leeson (whose policeman father trained him for the force by teaching him the straight left), with hundreds of other police drafted in from all parts of London, went through the Whitechapel doss-houses, clubs and courts. Wensley and Leeson had both picked up some Yiddish, through being in the East End, though much had to be done by means of interpreters in Russian, Polish, Latvian and many other languages. Detective Chief Inspector Nicholls, then a young City policeman, was employed on the same work.

> 'For several days none of us had our clothes off for any
> sleep. My own Christmas dinner in 1910 was some bread
> and butter and tea in an alley down Petticoat Lane way.'

Those few people who talked to them at all told lies.

They had better luck from informers who came privately. Svaars had had a girlfriend called Luba Milstein. Her brothers lived in London and hated Svaars. When a police description of a wanted woman was put out the brothers thought it was her and brought her in to Leman Street Police Station. Gardstein's own girlfriend became hysterical when she heard he was dead, and that he had been at Houndsditch, and she confessed to her landlord. He went to the police. In a parcel she had given to her landlord were photographs of herself and Gardstein.

Before Christmas the police had arrested five people, but they had not accounted for all those who had been at Houndsditch and they could not prove who had actually shot the policemen. But as information came in they began a series of raids on houses in Whitechapel and Stepney. All they usually had to go on was a name, often false, and a vague description. On one occasion they were a few minutes too late to catch three suspects, who fled to France.

On the evening of 1 January 1911 an unknown man came to the City Police headquarters and said that he knew where two wanted men were hiding. One was known only as 'Joseph'; the other was Fritz Svaars. It is likely that the informer was a landlord of rooms where they had lived earlier. They were at 100 Sidney Street, Stepney, living with a woman called Gershon. He also gave the police a letter from Svaars to friends in Russia, saying that as he would be hanged (if caught) he was going to commit suicide or shoot his way through the police. The crisis had come.

The battle of Sidney Street

The police were in no doubt about the danger of tackling these men, but there was no choice. They had to be caught before they disappeared once more. Superintendent Ottaway decided to bring his men into the area that night and go in on the morning of 2 January.

Metropolitan and City men were brought in from a wide area – and every one of them was single. When it was known that married policemen had not been chosen every man present realized that he might have less than one more day to live.

The local detective sergeant briefed the senior officers on the exact layout of Sidney Street. Detectives occupied the houses at the back of No. 100 and in the street opposite. Then they came quietly up to No. 100 itself. There were three families in the house besides the wanted men. A Yiddish-speaking interpreter knocked on the ground-floor window and roused the couple sleeping inside. Everyone in the house, including Mrs Gershon, was quietly brought out. She had let the two men stay in her room out of fear.

The police could not storm into the room, which was on the second floor, up a narrow staircase. No one would live to reach the door. Now the anarchists had the house to themselves. At 7.30 a.m. a shower of gravel was thrown against the first-floor

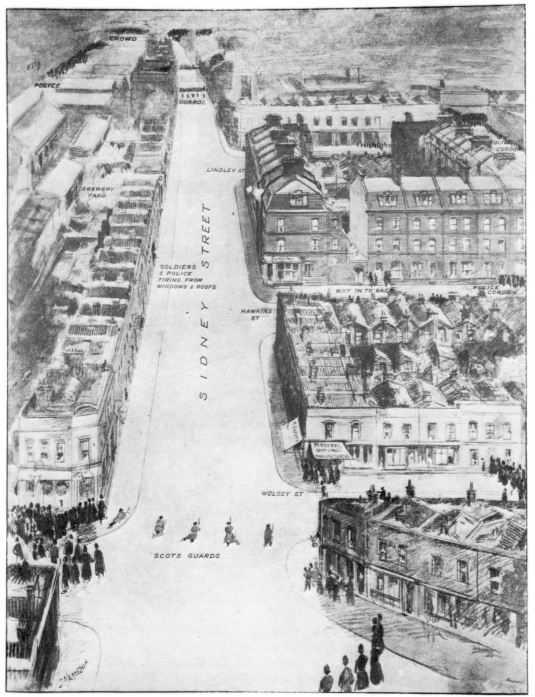

left: *This sketch from the* Graphic *gives a clear picture of the layout of Sidney Street. How would you have tried to arrest the anarchists? Their house was outlined in black by the artist.*

right: *While the guardsmen engage the anarchists the police try to keep back sightseers. The police cordon is visible at the further end of the street. It was thought that other anarchists might try to rescue the trapped men.*

window. The idea was to see if the gunmen could be 'talked out'. The reply was immediate: revolver fire. Police Sergeant Leeson was shot: 'The first shot passed through my right boot, injuring my foot. The second struck me just below the heart, passing through my lungs.' Other policemen and a doctor were pinned down by rapid firing, coming from various rooms in the house. The police had old-fashioned rifles, because they were so little used that no one had thought to supply up-to-date ones. The anarchists' modern Mauser pistols were much more deadly.

When the police are dealing with armed and dangerous men they can call in the army to help them. This was such a crisis and there was an urgent call to the Home Secretary. He not only gave permission but hurried along to Sidney Street to be on the scene. It was Winston Churchill, then at the beginning of his career in government.

Twenty Scots Guardsmen, wearing their long grey overcoats and peaked caps, came hurrying along from the Tower, where they had been on ceremonial duty. They took up positions in surrounding houses and in the street itself and began firing through the windows into each room. Svaars and Joseph fired back. A reporter present saw bullets

'raining upon it. As I looked I saw how they spat at the walls, how they ripped splinters from the door. The noise of battle was almost continuous. The heavy barking reports of Army rifles were followed by the sharp and lighter crack of pistol shots... As I watched, gripped by the horror and drama of it, I saw a sharp stabbing flash break through the garret window.'

The Guardsmen replied, pouring streams of bullets into the house.

Svaars and Joseph must have known that the end was near.

above: *Churchill at Sidney Street. Many people thought he only went to the scene as a publicity stunt. Note that the police have nothing more powerful than a shotgun.*

above right: *The funeral service for the London policemen murdered by terrorists in 1910 as drawn for* The Graphic.

At about 1 p.m. they set the house on fire. As the smoke drifted in the slight wind, every man waited, revolver or rifle at the ready, for the final rush as the two assassins, far from their homeland, came forth to die. The flames grew higher but the house was completely silent. Firemen arrived and Churchill had to order them not to go near. The house roof fell in. No one could have been alive. The firemen, soldiers and detectives went into No. 100. Two bodies were found beneath the debris of the burned house. Joseph had been shot, probably by a soldier's bullet. Svaars must have set light to the house and made no attempt to escape. He had suffocated to death. The battle was over.

Four other members of the gang were eventually arrested, but no one ever served a prison sentence. This was mainly because at their trial the prosecution thought that Gardstein, the man shot by his comrade, had committed the murder of the policemen, when in fact it was another member of the gang. The prisoners had to be given the benefit of the doubt, and were all eventually released. The man who most probably killed three London policemen went back to Russia and became a secret policeman himself. He was executed by Stalin in the 1930s.

8   The London police after eighty years

At the time of Sidney Street the London police still remained, in essentials, the force that Peel had created in 1829. His idea, a uniformed body of men out in the streets preventing crime, had not changed, even if some of them now patrolled on bicycles. His organization, too, with its divisions and beats, had hardly changed, though it had grown as London had spread, and now covered a far larger area. The C.I.D. had been a big innovation, perhaps, but its members were still using many of the same old cunning tricks the Bow Street Runners had known. Peel's work had stood the test of time.

Changes, though, had begun and were continuing, and some of them were to transform a great part of police work in the twentieth century. Scientific methods, especially the recording of finger-prints, were becoming established. The automobile had made its appearance, though none could foresee what a revolution it would bring about. A few women had been employed since 1907 to deal with difficulties involving women and girls, though it was to be another thirty years before regular policewomen were recruited. Just as conditions in other trades improved, so it was for the police: standards of education and chances of promotion rose, though it was 1958 before a man who had begun as an ordinary constable reached the very top, when Joseph Simpson was appointed Commissioner.

The most important change of all, though, had already taken place. It was in the attitude of ordinary people to the police. In 1833 P.C. Culley's murderers had been cheered by a coroner's jury. 'Down with the new police! Down with the raw lobsters, Peel's bloody gang!' But in 1910 three murdered policemen received a public funeral in St Paul's Cathedral, with everyone from the Lord Mayor to a large party of taxi-drivers coming to show their sympathy and support for the 'bobbies'. The police were not 'new' any more. They had become part of London itself.

The police forces of London

1829	**Metropolitan Police** First Commissioners, Charles Rowan and Richard Mayne. Headquarters, 4 Whitehall Place. About 3,300 in all.
1837	Mounted Police taken into Metropolitan force.
1839	**River Police.** Founded as private organization, 1798; taken into Metropolitan Police as Thames Division.
1839	End of Bow Street detectives.
1839	Metropolitan Police boundaries extended.
1839	**City of London Police** First Commissioner, Daniel Whittle Harvey.
1840	**Divisional Detectives**
1842	**'Scotland Yard' Detectives** At police headquarters, Whitehall Place.
1850	Rowan retires.
1856	First **Assistant Commissioners** appointed.
1862	Police strength now about 7,800 men.
1868	Mayne dies in office.
1878	**Detective Branch** reformed as **Criminal Investigation Department**
1882	Police strength about 11,700 men.
1883	**Special (Irish) Branch** set up.
1888	Police strength 14,200 men.
1889	Photography used to identify criminals.
1890	Move to New Scotland Yard.
1900	Police strength about 16,000 men.
1901	Police using bicycles.
1901	Sir Edward Henry develops finger-print system at Scotland Yard.
1910–11	Sidney Street siege.

'A part of the land-scape...' An ordinary London policeman on traffic duty in 1898.

Index

inspector, Metropolitan Police, 15, 21, 22
Ireland, 38
Irish Republican Brotherhood (Fenian Society), 38

Jack the Ripper, 25, 38
Justice of the Peace (J.P.), 4

Lansdowne, Detective Inspector, 28, 29
London Working Men's Committee, 36

magistrates, 4, 14
Marx, Karl, 40
Mayne, Richard, 12, 14-15, 19, 20, 23, 33, 36, 38
Metropolitan Police Force: founding of, 5, 12; headquarters of, 28; structure of, 12-13, 14-15, 27, 28

Nash, John, 9
National Union of the Working Classes, 36
Nicholas II (czar of Russia), 39
nicknames for police, 23
'night houses', 33

Parliament, 11, 12, 13
pay, police, 17, 18-19
Peel, Sir Robert, 12, 13, 17, 23, 24, 36, 47
pensions, police, 19
pickpockets, 9
Police Foundation, 20
poor, relations of, with police, 24
population increase, 5
prostitutes, 8, 25, 33
pubs, 8, 19

railways, 7-8
recruiting: of uniformed police, 15, 16, 17; of detectives, 29
refugees in London, 40, 41
Regent's Park, 9
Regent Street, 9
revolution, fear of, in England, 11
Revolution, French, 11
Riot Act, 37
riots, 11, 36; police action during, 36, 37-38
River Police, 10, 13, 23, 34-35
robberies, 4, 9, 21-22, 27
'Rogues Gallery', 35
Romany (gypsy language), 29
rookeries, 22, 29-32
Rowan, Charles, 12, 14, 15, 19
Russia, refugees from, in London, 41, 46

St Giles, 8, 11, 30, 31
St Katherine's Dock, 7
Scotland Yard, 28-29, 32, 34, 35, 38
sergeant, Metropolitan Police, 15, 17, 20, 21, 22, 29
Simpson, Joseph, 47
slang, thieves', 29
slums, 7, 8, 9, 11
Social Democratic Federation, 37
Special Branch (C.I.D.), 38-39, 41, 42
Stammers, Sergeant, 27
stations, railway, 7, 8
Stepney, 8, 9, 41
street venders, 8, 29
Superintendent of Police, 15, 17, 21, 22, 26, 29
Svaars, Fritz, 43
Sweeney, John, 38-39

telegraph, electric, 34

Thames, River, 7
turnover in police force, 26

Uniformed Branch of Metropolitan Police, 14-26
uniforms, police, 12, 15-16

Victoria (queen of England), 25, 39
Victoria Station, 8, 9
Vincent, Howard, 33, 34

Walker, Superintendent, 36-37
Warren, Sir Charles, 25, 38
watchmen, 4
Wellington, Duke of, 10
Wensley, Detective Inspector ('the Weasel'), 41, 43
West End, 9-10, 22, 33
West India Dock, 7, 10
Westminster, Duke of, 8, 9
Westminster Abbey, 27
Whitechapel, 8, 22, 25, 31-32, 41
Whitehall, 4, 28
Williamson, Superintendent Adolphus, 28, 29, 32

Acknowledgments

The author and publisher would like to thank the following for permission to reproduce illustrations:
Cover, p. 27 collection at Royal Holloway College, University of London; pp. 4, 11 Guildhall Library, City of London; p. 7 Port of London Authority; pp. 8, 9, 18, 21, 22, 23, 30, 33 (night house), 34, 37, 39, 40, 44, 46 (funeral) Cambridge University Library; pp. 10, 25, 26 Peter Jackson Collection; p. 12 National Portrait Gallery, London; pp. 14 (Rowan), 35 (river police) Metropolitan Police; pp. 14 (Mayne), 15, 16, 28, 45, 46 (Sidney Street Siege) Mansell Collection; pp. 20, 24, 35 (cartoon), 42 (Jewish immigrants) British Library Board; p. 31 British Museum and Weidenfeld & Nicolson Archives; pp. 32, 33 (Vincent) Radio Times Hulton Picture Library; p. 42 from W. J. Fishman, *Jewish Radicals*, Duckworth; p. 48 Kodak Museum.

The author also wishes to acknowledge his debt to the work of Kellow Chesney, *The Victorian Underworld*; Dr J. J. Tobias, *Crime and Industrial Society in the 19th Century* and *Nineteenth-Century Crime: Prevention and Punishment*; and Donald Rumbelow, whose *The Houndsditch Murders and the Siege of Sidney Street* has been used extensively in Chapter Seven. He would also like to thank the Librarian and staff of the Home Office Library, for research facilities.

Maps by Reg Piggott

New Scotland Yard. The famous building on the Thames Embankment was designed in the 'Victorian Gothic' style by Norman Shaw.

cover: 'The Railway Station', a painting by W. P. Frith of Paddington Station in 1862. Among the crowd on the platform are two detectives making an arrest.

The Cambridge History Library

The Cambridge Introduction to History
Written by Trevor Cairns

PEOPLE BECOME CIVILIZED

THE ROMANS AND THEIR EMPIRE

BARBARIANS, CHRISTIANS, AND MUSLIMS

THE MIDDLE AGES

EUROPE AND THE WORLD

THE BIRTH OF MODERN EUROPE

THE OLD REGIME AND THE REVOLUTION

POWER FOR THE PEOPLE

EUROPE AROUND THE WORLD

THE TWENTIETH CENTURY

The Cambridge Topic Books
General Editor Trevor Cairns

THE AMERICAN WAR OF INDEPENDENCE

THE AUTOMOBILE

BENIN: AN AFRICAN KINGDOM AND CULTURE

THE BUDDHA

BUILDING THE MEDIEVAL CATHEDRALS

CHINA AND MAO ZEDONG

CHRISTOPHER WREN
AND ST. PAUL'S CATHEDRAL

THE EARLIEST FARMERS AND THE FIRST CITIES

EARLY CHINA AND THE WALL

THE FIRST SHIPS AROUND THE WORLD

GANDHI AND THE STRUGGLE
FOR INDIA'S INDEPENDENCE

HERNAN CORTES: CONQUISTADOR IN MEXICO

HITLER AND THE GERMANS

THE INDUSTRIAL REVOLUTION BEGINS

LIFE IN A FIFTEENTH-CENTURY MONASTERY

LIFE IN A MEDIEVAL VILLAGE

LIFE IN THE IRON AGE

LIFE IN THE OLD STONE AGE

THE LONDON POLICE IN
THE NINETEENTH CENTURY

THE MAORIS

MARTIN LUTHER

MEIJI JAPAN

THE MURDER OF ARCHBISHOP THOMAS

MUSLIM SPAIN

THE NAVY THAT BEAT NAPOLEON

THE PARTHENON

POMPEII

THE PYRAMIDS

THE ROMAN ARMY

THE ROMAN ENGINEERS

ST. PATRICK AND IRISH CHRISTIANITY

THE VIKING SHIPS

Lerner Publications Company
241 First Avenue North, Minneapolis, Minnesota 55401